CPAG'S

Housing Benefit and Council Tax Benefit Legislation

29th Edition

2016/2017

Supplement

Commentary by
Carolyn George MA
Richard Poynter BCL, MA(Oxon), District Tribunal Judge, Judge of the Upper Tribunal
Stewart Wright MA, Dip. Law, Barrister, Judge of the Upper Tribunal
Martin Williams Welfare rights worker, CPAG
Susan Mitchell Freelance writer on welfare rights
Mark Brough Freelance writer on welfare rights

Statutory instruments up to date to **23 June 2017**

Published by CPAG, 30 Micawber Street, London N1 7TB

Child Poverty Action Group works on behalf of the one in four children in the UK growing up in poverty. It doesn't have to be like this. We use our understanding of what causes poverty and the impact it has on children's lives to campaign for policies that will prevent and solve poverty – for good. We provide training, advice and information to make sure hard-up families get the financial support they need. We also carry out high profile legal work to establish and protect families' rights. If you are not already supporting us, please consider making a donation, or ask for details of our membership schemes, training courses and publications.

Published by Child Poverty Action Group
30 Micawber Street, London N1 7TB
Tel: 020 7837 7979
staff@cpag.org.uk
www.cpag.org.uk

© Child Poverty Action Group 2017

This book is sold subject to the condition that it shall not, by way of trade or otherwise, be lent, resold, hired out or otherwise circulated without the publisher's prior consent in any form of binding or cover other than that in which it is published and without a similar condition including this condition being imposed on the subsequent purchaser.
A CIP record for this book is available from the British Library

Main work: ISBN 978 1 910715 11 6

Supplement: ISBN 978 1 910715 19 2

Child Poverty Action Group is a charity registered in England and Wales (registration number 294841) and in Scotland (registration number SC039339), and is a company limited by guarantee, registered in England (registration number 1993854). VAT number: 690 808117

Design by Devious Designs
Cover Design by Colorido Studios
Content management system by Konnect Soft www.konnectsoft.com
Typeset by David Lewis XML Associates Limited
Printed in the UK by CPI Goup (UK)

Contents

Introduction	iv
Table of cases	v
Table of Commissioners and Upper Tribunal decisions	v
How to use this supplement	vi

PART I: NOTER UP
1

PART II: SECONDARY LEGISLATION

The Council Tax Reduction (Scotland) Amendment (No.2) Regulations 2016 No.253	21
The Rent Officers (Housing Benefit and Universal Credit Functions) (Local Housing Allowance Amendments) Order 2016 No.1179	25
The Council Tax Reduction Schemes (Prescribed Requirements) (England) (Amendment) Regulations 2016 No.1262	29
The Council Tax Reduction Schemes (Prescribed Requirements and Default Scheme) (Wales) (Amendment) Regulations 2017 No.46 (W. 20)	34
The Council Tax Reduction (Scotland) Amendment Regulations 2017 No.41	44
The Valuation Tribunal for England (Council Tax and Rating Appeals) (Procedure) (Amendment) Regulations 2017 No.156	48
The Social Security (Income-Related Benefits) Amendment Regulations 2017 No.174	50
The Employment and Support Allowance and Universal Credit (Miscellaneous Amendments and Transitional and Savings Provisions) Regulations 2017 No.204	51
The Housing Benefit and Universal Credit (Size Criteria) (Miscellaneous Amendments) Regulations 2017 No.213	56
The Social Security (Scottish Infected Blood Support Scheme) Regulations 2017 No.329	61
The Social Security (Restrictions on Amounts for Children and Qualifying Young Persons) Amendment Regulations 2017 No.376	63
The Pensions Act 2014 (Consequential, Supplementary and Incidental Amendments) Order 2017 No.422	67
The Crown Estate Transfer Scheme 2017 No.524	69
The Employment and Support Allowance (Miscellaneous Amendments and Transitional and Savings Provision) Regulations 2017 No.581	70
The Social Security (Emergency Funds) (Amendment) Regulations 2017 No.689	72

Introduction

This Supplement to the 29th edition provides commentary on all relevant new caselaw and updates to the legislation to 23 June 2017.

Thanks to Nicola Johnston for editing and managing the production of this book and to Bryce Payton at David Lewis XML.

Comments on this Supplement and the main work are always welcomed and can be sent to the authors via CPAG.

Carolyn George, Richard Poynter, Stewart Wright, Martin Williams, Susan Mitchell and Mark Brough

Table of cases

Wilkinson v Chief Adjudication Officer, reported as *R(IS) 1/01*… **6**

Table of Commissioners' and Upper Tribunal decisions

AG v South Ayreshire Council (HB) [2017] UKUT 110 (AAC)… **18**
Babergh DC v GW (HB) [2017] UKUT 40 (AAC)… **4**
Bristol CC v JKT [2016] UKUT 517 (AAC)… **3, 4**
E v Dacorum BC & M [2017] UKUT 93 (AAC)… **7**
FK v Wandsworth BC (HB) [2016] UKUT 570 (AAC)… **4**
JM v Eastleigh BC [2016] UKUT 464 (AAC)… **6**
MMcF v Sefton BC (HB) [2016] UKUT 403 (AAC)… **18**
MW v SSWP (JSA) [2016] UKUT 469 (AAC)… **6**
R(H) 7/07… **18**
SSWP v Carmichael and Sefton BC (HB) [2017] UKUT 174 (AAC)… **5**

How to use this supplement

Use the Noter-up to find out about changes to the main volume. The page numbers on the left refer to pages in the main volume. The entry opposite either states what the change is or refers to another part of this supplement where the amending legislation is set out.

For abbreviations, see pxli of the main volume.

PART I:

NOTER UP

Noter-up

Welfare Reform Act 2012

New orders amend and modify provisions for claims and awards of universal credit, and amend previous commencement orders (including amendments to the Gateway Conditions for some claimants and removal of Gateway Conditions in some post code areas). See p1766 of the current edition for a list of the commencement orders made at the time that edition was written. The new orders are as follows:

From 1, 8 and 22 February, 8, 15, 22 and 29 March and 5, 12, 19 and 26 April 2017: The Welfare Reform Act 2012 (Commencement No.11, 13, 16, 22, 23 and 24 and Transitional and Transitory Provisions (Modification)) Order 2017 SI No.57. Articles 17, 18 and 19 modify the No.22 Order, the No.24 Order and the No.23 Order respectively.

From 6 April 2017: The Welfare Reform Act 2012 (Commencement No.9 and 21 and Transitional and Transitory Provisions (Amendment)) Order 2017 SI No.483, among other things, amends the No.21 Order (see p1792 of the current edition) in respect of transitional provisions for claims for HB.

From 3, 10 and 24 May and 7, 14 and 28 June: The Welfare Reform Act 2012 (Commencement No.19, 22, 23 and 24 and Transitional and Transitory Provisions (Modification)) Order 2017 SI No.584 modifies the No.19 Order, the No.22 Order, the No.23 Order and the No.24 Order.

pp224-46   **HB Regs reg 2 – Interpretation**

Definition of "Crown tenant" amended by Sch 5 para 102(a), and definition of "relevant person" inserted after definition of "relevant information" by Sch 5 para 102(b), of SI 2017 No.524 as from 31 March 2017.

Definitions of "the London Emergencies Trust" inserted after definition of "the London Bombings Relief Charitable Fund" and "the We Love Manchester Emergency Fund" inserted after the definition of "water charges", and definition of "qualifying person" amended, by reg 6(2) of SI 2017 No.689 as from 19 June 2017.

Definition of "the main phase employment and support allowance" amended by reg 5(2)(a) of SI 2017 No.581 as from 23 June 2017, subject to transitional and savings provision in reg 9.

Definition of "member of a couple who cannot share a bedroom" and paragraph (6) inserted, and para (a)(iii) of definition of "person who requires overnight care" amended, by reg 4(2) of SI 2017 No.213 as from 1 April 2017.

Definition of "member of the work-related activity group" inserted by Sch 1 para 6(2) of SI 2017 No.204 as from 3 April 2017, subject to transitional and savings provisions in Sch 2 paras 1–7.

Definition of "member of the work-related activity group" amended by reg 5(2)(b) of SI 2017 No.581 as from 23 June 2017, subject to transitional and savings provision in reg 9.

Definition of "qualifying person" amended, and definition of "Scottish Infected Blood Support Scheme" inserted, by reg 6(2) of SI 2017 No.329 as from 3 April 2017.

[p238: In the analysis of the definition of "close relative", before the sentence starting "the term "couple"...", add:]

In *Bristol CC v JKT* [2016] UKUT 517 (AAC), Judge Ward decided that half-brothers and half-sisters come within the definition of "close relative", although not expressly included. He said:

"The inclusion of step-parent and step-son/daughter can be seen as an acknowledgement of the relationship between the child's actual parent and his/her new partner and the role of that in creating bonds of a degree of closeness. The importance of the role of the relationship between partners in the definition can be seen in the extension of the provisions to "the other member of a couple". The legislator did not see fit to include step-brothers and step-sisters, the degree of whose connection via the relationship between their respective parents is one degree more remote. The tribunal judge considered that step-siblings and half-siblings might be in "quite a similar position", but whilst I accept that family relationships are infinitely various, it is a question of drawing a line somewhere and a rationale for the inclusion of the "step" provisions so far as they go is in my view, for the reason above, apparent. "Step" relationships were considered by the legislator to require express inclusion, as were relationships by marriage. The argument that relationships of the half blood also do is not made out when, as noted by Mr Commissioner Rice at para 5 of *R(SB) 22/87*, as a use of language it is indeed possible to refer to a half-brother as a "brother", even if in contexts where specificity is demanded "half-brother" might be used."

pp254-70   **HB Regs reg 7 – Circumstances in which a person is or is not to be treated as occupying a dwelling as his home**
Para (8)(c)(ii) amended by reg 5(3) of SI 2017 No.581 as from 23 June 2017, subject to transitional and savings provision in reg 9.

pp270-77   **HB Regs reg 8 – Circumstances in which a person is to be treated as liable to make payments in respect of a dwelling**

[p272: In the analysis of paragraph (1), at the end of the paragraph numbered (2), add:]

The use of the term "reasonable" within regulation 8(1)(c)(ii) means reasonable in all the circumstances and in light of the overall purpose of the HB scheme: *FK v Wandsworth BC (HB)* [2016] UKUT 570 (AAC); *Babergh DC v GW (HB)* [2017] UKUT 40 (AAC).

[p274: In the analysis of the term "liable", after the quote ending "... otherwise erred in law", add a new paragraph:]

In *FK v Wandsworth BC (HB)* [2016] UKUT 570 (AAC), the claimant lived in a property that was the sole tenancy of her sister, without the agreement of the landlord. Her sister had not intended to live in, and had never lived in, the property, renting it only to enable the claimant to obtain accommodation. The First-tier Tribunal decided that the arrangement between the claimant and her sister did not create a legal liability – ie, that the claimant was not entitled to HB because she was not liable to make payments in respect of the dwelling to the landlord or her sister. Judge Hemingway decided that the tribunal had not erred in this regard, but it had, in failing to go on to consider whether the claimant could be treated as liable under reg 8(1)(c)(ii) – ie, if she had to make the payments to continue to live in the dwelling because the liable person (her sister) was not doing so and it was reasonable to treat her as liable. The judge pointed out that there is an argument that where there is dishonesty, it will not necessarily be appropriate to conclude that it is reasonable to treat a claimant as liable under reg 8(1)(c). He said:

> "... the use of the term "reasonable" within regulation 8(1)(c)(ii) is to be regarded as meaning reasonable in all the circumstances and in light of the overall purpose of the housing benefit scheme. That was the way in which I think Commissioner Mesher (as he then was) had approached the matter in CH/3013/2003 (see in particular paragraph 34 of that decision). Looked at in that way, although I was concerned about the point when I granted permission, it does not seem to me it can properly be said that any dishonesty either on the part of a claimant or on the part of someone intimately involved with the process of claiming (perhaps in this case *[the claimant's sister]*) should necessarily lead to a conclusion that it would not be reasonable to treat a claimant as being liable. Rather, such might be regarded as one of many factors which may have relevance to that question."

The judge in *Babergh DC v GW (HB)* [2017] UKUT 40 (AAC) agreed.

pp277-93   **HB Regs reg 9 – Circumstances in which a person is to be treated as not liable to make payments in respect of a dwelling**

[p284: In the analysis of paragraph (1)(b) and (8), in the paragraph starting "Close relative", after the third sentence, add:]

See also the discussion of *Bristol CC v JKT* [2016] UKUT 517 (AAC) on p238.

pp360-67   **HB Regs reg B13 – Determination of maximum rent (social sector)**
Percentages in para (3)(a) and (b) confirmed by art 22(2) of SI 2017 No.260 as from 1 April 2017 (3 April 2017 where rent payable weekly or in multiples of a week).

Para (5)(za) and (zb) inserted, para (5)(a) amended, para (6)(a) and (ab) substituted, para (7)(b) amended, and para (9)(e) inserted by reg 4(3) of SI 2017 No.213 as from 1 April 2017. The substituted para (6)(a) subsequently amended by correction slip dated 15 March 2017.

[p367: In the analysis of paragraphs (6) and (7), after the paragraph starting "the Court found against all the other claimants ...", add a new paragraph:]

As well as seeking a judicial review, Mr Carmichael had appealed to the First-tier Tribunal against the local authority's decision to calculate his HB with a reduction of 14 per cent under para (3)(a). A three-judge panel dealt with the Secretary of State's appeal to the Upper Tribunal in *SSWP v Carmichael and Sefton BC (HB)* [2017] UKUT 174 (AAC). A lead case in more than 200 appeals, it considered the powers of the First-tier Tribunal where the ordinary application of the words of secondary legislation results in an undisputed breach of a claimant's Convention rights under the Human Rights Act 1998. The First-tier Tribunal had found in Mr Carmichael's favour. To avoid a breach of Convention rights it had read words into reg B13(5)(a) (the "size criteria") to the effect that no 14 per cent reduction applied in Mr Carmichael's case. The Upper Tribunal decided that it should not have done so, but should have instead directed the local authority to calculate his HB without making a deduction of 14 per cent, giving the same outcome. It said:

"We conclude that in such cases, and in the light of *Mathieson* [*Mathieson v Secretary of State for Work and Pensions* [2015] UKSC 47] and similar authorities discussed below, courts and tribunals ultimately have the power to determine and so order or direct that to the extent that subordinate legislation is incompatible with a person's Convention rights it should not be given effect to in determining the person's lawful entitlement, or should be otherwise applied or disapplied in a way that does not breach the person's Convention rights. In our judgment that is a "relief or remedy" which a court or tribunal may make "within its powers as it considers just and appropriate" under section 8(1) of the 1998 Act. Indeed, an analogous power exists at common law, predating the 1998 Act (see *R v Lord Chancellor ex parte Witham* [1998] 2 WLR 849). For a court, especially one exercising the discretionary judicial review jurisdiction, it may be sufficient to make a declaration to the effect that the individual's rights have been breached. Statutory tribunals, however, are charged with making an actual decision on a person's lawful benefit entitlement."

Thus the Secretary of State's appeal was allowed but the Upper Tribunal made a decision to the same effect as the First-tier Tribunal. The Upper Tribunal refused the Secretary of State's application for leave to appeal to the Court of Appeal, but suspended the effect of its decision pending an application for permission direct to the Court.

pp375-83   HB Regs reg 13D – Determination of a maximum rent (LHA)
Para (3)(za) and (zb) inserted, para (3)(a) and the closing words of para (3) amended and para (3A)(a) substituted by reg 4(4) of SI 2017 No.213 as from 1 April 2017.

pp397-98   HB Regs reg 22 – Applicable amounts
Sub-para (e) amended by Sch 1 para 6(3) of SI 2017 No.204 as from 3 April 2017, subject to transitional and savings provisions in Sch 2 paras 1–7.

Sub-para (b) amended, the existing text of the reg designated para (1) and paras (2)–(5) inserted by reg 7(2) of SI 2017 No.376 as from 6 April 2017, subject to transitional provision in reg 9.

pp398-99   HB Regs reg 23 – Polygamous marriages
Sub-para (f) amended by Sch 1 para 6(4) of SI 2017 No.204 as from 3 April 2017, subject to transitional and savings provisions in Sch 2 paras 1–7.

Sub-para (c) amended, the existing text of the reg designated para (1) and paras (2)–(5) inserted by reg 7(2) of SI 2017 No.376 as from 6 April 2017, subject to transitional provision in reg 9.

pp406-8   HB Regs reg 27 – Calculation of income on a weekly basis
Amounts in para (3)(a) and (b) confirmed by art 22(3) of SI 2017 No.260 as from 1 April 2017 (3 April 2017 where rent payable weekly or in multiples of a week).

Noter-up

pp409-10   HB Regs reg 28 – Treatment of child care charges
Para (11)(a) and (ba) amended by Sch 1 para 6(5) of SI 2017 No.204 as from 3 April 2017, subject to transitional and savings provisions in Sch 2 paras 1–7.

pp436-43   HB Regs reg 42 – Notional income
Para (7)(a) amended by reg 6(3)(a) of SI 2017 No.329 as from 3 April 2017 and by reg 6(3)(a) of SI 689 as from 19 June 2017.

pp443-61   HB Regs Part 6, Section 6 – Capital

[p443: In the General Note on Section 6, in the paragraph starting "It is important...", before the sentence starting "Likewise, if a claimant...", insert:]

In *MW v SSWP (JSA)* [2016] UKUT 469 (AAC), similar questions arose in respect of entitlement to income-based JSA for a claimant who had been lent £20,000 by his mother for the purpose of buying his home. Given the obligation to repay the funds if not used for that specific purpose, the claimant's situation in Scots Private Law was held to be analogous to holding the sum on trust and it did not fall to be considered as the claimant's capital.

pp445-47   HB Regs reg 46 – Income treated as capital
Para (6) amended by reg 6(3)(b) of SI 2017 No.329 as from 3 April 2017 and by reg 6(3)(b) of SI 2017 No.689 as from 19 June 2017.

p449   HB Regs reg 49 – Notional capital
Para (4)(a) amended by reg 6(3)(c) of SI 2017 No.329 as from 3 April 2017 and by reg 6(3)(c) of SI 2017 No.689 as from 19 June 2017.

pp458-59   HB Regs reg 51 – Capital jointly held

[p459: After the paragraph which starts "The "value of half" approach has...", insert a new paragraph:]

In *JM v Eastleigh BC* [2016] UKUT 464 (AAC), Judge Jacobs stated that this is perhaps too pessimistic a view of the possibilities of realising the value of a part share in a property. He cited the decision of the Court of Appeal in *Wilkinson v Chief Adjudication Officer*, reported as *R(IS) 1/01*, which was decided on the equivalent provisions in income support legislation. The value of the claimant's share depends simply on whether it can be realised, and not on the difficulties those who held the other shares in the property may have in buying the claimant's share. Whether it can be realised depends on the circumstances of each case, but Judge Jacobs noted that there is increased awareness of markets that exist for investors in such shares.

pp496-98   HB Regs reg 74 – Non-dependant deductions
Para (8)(a) amended by Sch 1 para 6(6) of SI 2017 No.204 as from 3 April 2017, subject to transitional and savings provisions in Sch 2 paras 1–7.

Para (8)(a) amended by reg 5(4) of SI 2017 No.581 as from 23 June 2017, subject to transitional and savings provision in reg 9.

Amounts in paras (1)(a) and (b) and (2)(a)–(e) amended by art 22(4) of SI 2017 No.260 as from 1 April 2017 (3 April 2017 where rent payable weekly or in multiples of a week).

Para (9)(b) amended by reg 6(3)(d) of SI 2017 No.329 as from 3 April 2017 and by reg 6(3)(d) of SI 2017 No.689 as from 19 June 2017.

pp533-36   HB Regs reg 86 – Evidence and information
Para (4)(a)(ii) amended by reg 6(3)(e) of SI 2017 No.329 as from 3 April 2017 and by reg 6(3)(e) of SI 2017 No.689 as from 19 June 2017.

pp554-37   HB Regs reg 96 – Circumstances in which payment may be made to a landlord

[p556: Before the paragraph which starts "Para (2) enables...", insert a new paragraph:]

In *E v Dacorum BC & M* [2017] UKUT 93 (AAC), Judge Mitchell considered the circumstances in which sub-para (c) applies. In that case, a tenant had been evicted for non-payment of rent. The payment of subsequent arrears of HB to the landlord to clear outstanding rent arrears was disputed by the tenant. Judge Mitchell emphasised that sub-para (c) does not give an unrestricted power to authorities to pay arrears of HB to a landlord in such circumstances. The authority must be satisfied that there are outstanding payments of rent, and payment to a landlord is limited to the amount of those arrears. The amount may be reduced by factors such as whether a deposit was retained, depending on the terms of the lease in regard to the purpose of the deposit. In the absence of specific contractual terms, other costs, such as those incurred by the landlord to secure eviction, cannot be added to the outstanding rent. Outstanding rent may be reduced by any costs incurred by the tenant that s/he would be likely to succeed in having taken into account had s/he faced an action for recovery of rent arrears.

pp587-90   HB Regs reg 114A – Information to be provided to rent officers

Para (9)(ca) amended by reg 4(5) of SI 2017 No.213 as from 1 April 2017.

pp597-602   HB Regs Sch 1 – Ineligible service charges

Amounts in para 2(2)(a) and (b)(i) and (ii), 2(3)(a) and (b)(i) and (ii), and 2(5) amended by art 22(5), and amounts in para 6(2)(a)–(d) confirmed by art 22(6), of SI 2017 No.260 as from 1 April 2017 (3 April 2017 where rent payable weekly or in multiples of a week).

pp602-07   HB Regs Sch 2 – Excluded tenancies

Para 2(3)(f) and (h) amended by reg 4(6) of SI 2017 No.213 as from 1 April 2017.

pp607-30   HB Regs Sch 3 – Applicable amounts

Paras 1, 2(1), 4 and 30(4) amended by reg 7(4) of SI 2017 No.376 as from 6 April 2017, subject to transitional provision in reg 9.

Para 1A(a) amended by reg 5(5) of SI 2017 No.581 as from 23 June 2017, subject to transitional and savings provision in reg 9.

Amounts in the table in para 2(1) confirmed by art 22(7) and Sch 5, amounts in para 20(5)–(9) amended by art 22(9) and Sch 6, and amount in para 26 amended by art 22(10), of SI 2017 No.260 as from 1 April 2017 (3 April 2017 where rent payable weekly or in multiples of a week).

The introductory words and sub-paras (b) and (c)(ii) of para 21(1), and para 22(2), amended, and paras 23 and 25 omitted, by Sch 1 para 6(7) of SI 2017 No.204 as from 3 April 2017, subject to transitional and savings provisions in Sch 2 paras 1–7.

pp631-40   HB Regs Sch 4 – Sums to be disregarded in the calculation of earnings

Paras 3(2) and 17(2)(b)(iv)(aa) and (bb) and the closing words of sub-para (iv) amended by Sch 1 para 6(8) of SI 2017 No.204 as from 3 April 2017, subject to transitional and savings provisions in Sch 2 paras 1–7.

Amounts in para 17(1) and (3)(c) confirmed by art 22(11) of SI 2017 No.260 as from 1 April 2017 (3 April 2017 where rent payable weekly or in multiples of a week).

Para 17(2)(b)(iv)(bb) amended by reg 5(6) of SI 2017 No.581 as from 23 June 2017, subject to transitional and savings provision in reg 9.

pp640-57   HB Regs Sch 5 – Sums to be disregarded in the calculation of income other than earnings

Para 15(g) substituted by reg 5 of SI 2017 No.174 as from 20 March 2017.

Para 35(1) and (7) amended by reg 6(3)(f) of SI 2017 No.329 as from 3 April 2017 and by reg 6(3)(f) of SI 2017 No.689 as from 19 June 2017.

Noter-up

Amount in para 56 confirmed by art 22(12) of SI 2017 No.260 as from 1 April 2017 (3 April 2017 where rent payable weekly or in multiples of a week).

Para 67 inserted by art 25(2) of SI 2017 No.422 as from 6 April 2017, subject to transitional provisions in arts 2 and 3.

pp657-73   HB Regs Sch 6 – Capital to be disregarded
Para 9(1)(h) inserted by art 25(3)(a), and para 62 inserted by art 25(3)(b), of SI 2017 No.422 as from 6 April 2017, subject to transitional provisions in arts 2 and 3.

Paras 24(1) and (7) and 34 amended by reg 6(3)(g) of SI 2017 No.329 as from 3 April 2017

Para 24(1) and (7) by reg 6(3)(g) of SI 2017 No.689 as from 19 June 2017.

pp690-702   HB (SPC) Regs reg 2 – Interpretation
Definition of "Crown tenant" amended (as reg 2 applies in relation to Scotland) by Sch 5 para 103(a), and definition of "relevant person" inserted (as reg 2 applies in relation to Scotland) after definition of "relevant information" by Sch 5 para 103(b), of SI 2017 No.524 as from 31 March 2017.

Definitions of "the London Emergencies Trust" inserted after definition of "the London Bombings Relief Charitable Fund" and "the We Love Manchester Emergency Fund" inserted after the definition of "water charges" and definition of "qualifying person" amended by reg 7(2) of SI 2017 No.689 as from 19 June 2017.

Definition of "the main phase employment and support allowance" amended by reg 6(2)(a) of SI 2017 No.581 as from 23 June 2017, subject to transitional and savings provision in reg 9.

Definition of "member of a couple who cannot share a bedroom" and paragraph (7) inserted, and para (a)(iii) of definition of "person who requires overnight care" amended, by reg 5(2) of SI 2017 No.213 as from 1 April 2017.

Definition of "member of the work-related activity group" inserted by Sch 1 para 7(2) of SI 2017 No.204 as from 3 April 2017, subject to transitional and savings provisions in Sch 2 paras 1–7.

Definition of "member of the work-related activity group" amended by reg 6(2)(b) of SI 2017 No.581 as from 23 June 2017, subject to transitional and savings provision in reg 9.

Definition of "qualifying person" amended, and definition of "Scottish Infected Blood Support Scheme" inserted, by reg 7(2) of SI 2017 No.329 as from 3 April 2017.

pp724-27   HB (SPC) Regs reg 13D – Determination of a maximum rent (LHA)
Para (3)(za) and (zb) inserted, para (3)(a) and the closing words of para (3) amended, and para (3A)(a) substituted by reg 5(3) of SI 2017 No.213 as from 1 April 2017.

pp733-34   HB (SPC) Regs reg 22 – Applicable amounts
Para (1)(b) amended, and paras (5A)–(5D) inserted, by reg 8(2) of SI 2017 No.376 as from 6 April 2017, subject to transitional provision in reg 9.

pp737-40   HB (SPC) Regs reg 29 – Meaning of "income"
Para (1)(j)(xiii) substituted by art 26(2) of SI 2017 No.422 as from 6 April 2017, subject to transitional provisions in arts 2 and 3.

Para (1)(m) substituted by reg 6(2) of SI 2017 No.174 as from 20 March 2017.

pp740-41   HB (SPC) Regs reg 30 – Calculation of income on a weekly basis
Amounts in para (3)(a) and (b) confirmed by art 23(2) of SI 2017 No.260 as from 1 April 2017 (3 April 2017 where rent payable weekly or in multiples of a week).

pp741-45   HB (SPC) Regs reg 31 – Treatment of child care charges
Para (11)(ba) amended by Sch 1 para 7(3) of SI 2017 No.204 as from 3 April 2017, subject to transitional and savings provisions in Sch 2 paras 1–7.

Noter-up

pp768-70   HB (SPC) Regs reg 55 – Non-dependant deductions
Para (8) amended by Sch 1 para 7(4) of SI 2017 No.204 as from 3 April 2017, subject to transitional and savings provisions in Sch 2 paras 1–7. Amounts in paras (1)(a) and (b) and (2)(a)–(e) amended by art 23(3) of SI 2017 No.260 as from 1 April 2017 (3 April 2017 where rent payable weekly or in multiples of a week).

Para (8) amended by reg 6(3) of SI 2017 No.581 as from 23 June 2017, subject to transitional and savings provision in reg 9.

Para (10)(b) amended by reg 7(3)(a) of SI 2017 No.329 as from 3 April 2017 and by reg 7(3)(a) of SI 2017 No.689 as from 19 June 2017.

pp784-85   HB (SPC) Regs reg 67 – Evidence and information
Para (4)(a)(ii) amended by reg 7(3)(b) of SI 2017 No.329 as from 3 April 2017 and by reg 7(3)(b) of SI 2017 No.689 as from 19 June 2017.

pp802-05   HB (SPC) Regs reg 95A – Information to be provided to rent officers
Para (9)(ba) amended by reg 5(4) of SI 2017 No.213 as from 1 April 2017.

pp809-12   HB (SPC) Regs Sch 1 – Ineligible service charges
Amounts in para 2(2)(a) and (b)(i) and (ii), 2(3)(a) and (b)(i) and (ii), and 2(5) amended by art 23(4), and amounts in para 6(2)(a)–(d) confirmed by art 23(5), of SI 2017 No.260 as from 1 April 2017 (3 April 2017 where rent payable weekly or in multiples of a week).

pp812-14   HB (SPC) Regs Sch 2 – Excluded tenancies
Para 2(2)(e) and (f) amended by reg 5(5) of SI 2017 No.213 as from 1 April 2017.

pp815-20   HB (SPC) Regs Sch 3 – Applicable amounts
Amounts in the table in para 1 amended, and amounts in the table in para 2(1) confirmed, by art 23(6) and Sch 7, and amounts in the table in para 12 amended by para 23(8) and Sch 8, of SI 2017 No.260 as from 1 April 2017 (3 April 2017 where rent payable weekly or in multiples of a week).

pp820-23   HB (SPC) Regs Sch 4 – Sums disregarded from claimant's earnings
Para 5(1)(d)(ii) amended by Sch 1 para 7(5) of SI 2017 No.204 as from 3 April 2017, subject to transitional and savings provisions in Sch 2 paras 1–7.

Amounts in para 9(1) and (3)(c) confirmed by art 23(9) of SI 2017 No.260 as from 1 April 2017 (3 April 2017 where rent payable weekly or in multiples of a week).

pp823-28   HB (SPC) Regs Sch 5 – Amounts to be disregarded in the calculation of income other than earnings
Para 1(g) substituted by reg 6(3) of SI 2017 No.174 as from 20 March 2017.

Amount in para 21 confirmed by art 23(10) of SI 2017 No.260 as from 1 April 2017 (3 April 2017 where rent payable weekly or in multiples of a week).

pp828-35   HB (SPC) Regs Sch 6 – Capital to be disregarded
Para 16(1)(a) amended by reg 7(3)(c) of SI 2017 No.329 as from 3 April 2017 and by reg 7(3)(c) of SI 2017 No.689 as from 19 June 2017.

Para 21(2)(p) inserted by art 26(3)(a), and para 26H inserted by art 26(3)(b), of SI 2017 No.422 as from 6 April 2017, subject to transitional provisions in arts 2 and 3.

pp850-51   The Rent Officers (Housing Benefit Functions) Order 1997 art 4B – Broad rental market area determinations and local housing allowance determinations
Para (1B) inserted by art 2(2) of SI 2016 No.1179 as from 23 January 2017.

pp863-64   The Rent Officers (Housing Benefit Functions) Order 1997 Sch 2 – Size criteria
Sub paras (za) and (zb) inserted in para 1, sub-para (a) and the closing words of para 1 amended, para 1A(a) substituted, and para 3 amended by reg 2 of SI 2017 No.213 as from 1 April 2017.

Noter-up

pp865-67   **The Rent Officers (Housing Benefit Functions) Order 1997 Sch 3B – Broad rental market area determinations and local housing allowance determinations**
Sub-paras (2A) and (2B) inserted, sub-para (3) amended and sub-para (3A) inserted in para 2 by art 2(3)(a), and para 5A inserted by art 2(3)(b) of SI 2016 No.1179 as from 23 January 2017.

pp872-73   **The Rent Officers (Housing Benefit Functions) (Scotland) Order 1997 art 4B – Broad rental market area determinations and local housing allowance determinations**
Para (1B) inserted by art 3(2) of SI 2016 No.1179 as from 23 January 2017.

p884   **The Rent Officers (Housing Benefit Functions) (Scotland) Order 1997 Sch 2 – Size criteria**
Sub paras (za) and (zb) inserted in para 1, sub-para (a) and the closing words of para 1 amended, para 1A(a) substituted, and para 3 amended by reg 3 of SI 2017 No.213 as from 1 April 2017.

pp885-87   **The Rent Officers (Housing Benefit Functions) (Scotland) Order 1997 Sch 3B – Broad rental market area determinations and local housing allowance determinations**
Sub-paras (2A) and (2B) inserted, sub-para (3) amended and sub-para (3A) inserted in para 2 by art 3(3) of SI 2016 No.1179 as from 23 January 2017.

pp911-17   **D & A Regs reg 7 – Decisions superseding earlier decisions**
Para (2)(o)(iv)(bb) amended by Sch 1 para 4 of SI 2017 No.204 as from 3 April 2017, subject to transitional and savings provisions in Sch 2 paras 1–7.

pp1031-34   **LGFA 1992 s13A – Reductions by billing authority**
[p1034: In the paragraph which begins "Authorities must consider…", after "para 14;" replace "Valuation Tribunal for England Practice Statement A11 Council Tax Reduction Appeals, para 27." with "Valuation Tribunal for England Consolidated Practice Statement 2017 (VTE CPS 2017), PS6, para 17 (which replaced Valuation Tribunal for England Practice Statement A11 Council Tax Reduction Appeals, para 27)".]

[p1034: In the paragraph which begins "In SC v East Riding of Yorkshire Council…", replace from "The Practice Statement was therefore amended" to the end of the paragraph with:]

Practice Statement A11 was therefore amended to state that a tribunal is not restricted to inquiring whether the billing authority has exercised its discretion lawfully and reasonably but must consider an appeal on its merits and may substitute its view for that of the authority (if there are sound reasons for doing so): *Practice Statement A11*, para 28; see also *SC v East Riding of Yorkshire Council*, para 24. This revised version of Practice Statement A11 has now been replaced by *VTE CPS* 2017, PS6 and the above information has been reproduced in *VTE CPS* 2017, PS6, para 18.

[p1034: In the paragraph which begins "The President outlined…" at the end of the first sentence delete "; Practice Statement A11, Annex 6".]

pp1035-37   **LGFA 1992 s16 – Appeals General**
[p1036: In the paragraph which begins "In England, at the request of the VTE President…", replace "CTR appeals on the assessment of income or capital or on the right of residence should be listed before a judge of the First-tier Tribunal and a senior member of the Valuation Tribunal: Practice Statement A11: Council Tax Reduction Appeals, para 33." with:]

The President may only request this if he thinks that the First-tier Tribunal members are likely to have particular expertise that is relevant to the determination of the appeal, or to appeals of its kind.

[p1036: Replace the paragraph which begins "In addition, any other case…" with:]

In addition, any other case raising "a novel, important, difficult or contentious point of law" must be referred to the registrar who will consult with the President about whether it should be listed for

Noter-up

hearing by the President, a Vice President or a panel of the Valuation Tribunal for England in accordance with Valuation Tribunal for England Consolidated Practice Statement 2017 (VTE CPS 2017), PS6, para 23.

[p1037: Delete the paragraph which begins "The judge of the First-tier Tribunal…".]

pp1059-66 The Council Tax Reduction Schemes (Prescribed Requirements) (England) Regulations 2012 reg 2 – Interpretation

Definition of "member of the work-related activity group" inserted by Sch 1 para 8(2) of SI 2017 No.204 as from 3 April 2017, subject to transitional and savings provisions in Sch 2 paras 1–7.

Definition of "Scottish basic rate" and "Scottish taxpayer" inserted by reg 2(2) of SI 2016 No.1262 as from 15 January 2017, in relation to schemes made for financial years starting on or after 1 April 2017.

pp1074-106 The Council Tax Reduction Schemes (Prescribed Requirements) (England) Regulations 2012 Sch 1 – Pensioners: matters that must be included in an authority's scheme

In para 5, sub-paras (2)(a)–(c) amended and (d) inserted, sub-paras (2A)–(2F) inserted, sub-paras (3)(a) substituted and (3)(c), (d), (e) and (g) amended, sub-paras (3A)–(3G) inserted and in sub-para (6) definitions of "continental shelf worker", "designated area", "mariner", "member of Her Majesty's forces posted overseas" and "prescribed area" inserted by reg 2(3)(a) of SI 2016 No.1262 as from 15 January 2017 in relation to schemes made for financial years starting on or after 1 April 2017, subject to transitional provision in reg 3.

Amounts in para 8(1)(a) and (b) and (2)(a)–(c) amended by reg 2(3)(b), para 19(5)(a) amended by reg 2(3)(c), para 28(aa) inserted and (b) amended by reg 2(3)(d) and para 30(1)(b) and (2) amended by reg 2(3)(e) of SI 2016 No.1262 as from 15 January 2017 in relation to schemes made for financial years starting on or after 1 April 2017.

Para 16(1)(j)(xiii) substituted by art 41 of SI 2017 No.422 as from 6 April 2017, subject to transitional provisions in arts 2 and 3.

Para 25(10)(c) amended by Sch 1 para 8(3) of SI 2017 No.204 as from 3 April 2017, subject to transitional and savings provisions in Sch 2 paras 1–7.

[p1077: In the General Note to Sch 1 para 5, at the start of the third sentence, replace "A period of temporary absence" with:]

Subject to the transitional provision in reg 3 of SI 2016 No.1262, "a period of temporary absence"

[p1077: In the General Note to Sch 1 para 5, in the third sentence before "13 or 52 weeks" insert "4" and in the final sentence of the General Note delete from ", there is not the same distinction" to "outside Great Britain,".]

[p1078: In the General Note to Sch 1 para 6, at the end of the second sentence after "commentary", add:]

but note that council tax reduction schemes for pensioners should not place a restriction on the number of children for whom you can receive an amount under Sch 2 para 2 (ie, the so called 'two-child limit', which in some circumstances applies to HB, does not apply to CTR for pensioners).

pp1106-11 The Council Tax Reduction Schemes (Prescribed Requirements) (England) Regulations 2012 Sch 2 – Amounts of alternative maximum council tax reduction

Amounts in column (2) of the table in para 1 amended by reg 2(4)(a), and amounts in the table after para 11 amended by reg 2(4)(b), of SI 2016 No.1262 as from 15 January 2017, in relation to schemes made for financial years starting on or after 1 April 2017.

pp1111-12 The Council Tax Reduction Schemes (Prescribed Requirements) (England) Regulations 2012 Sch 3 – Applicable amounts

Amounts in sub-para (b)(i) and (ii) in the table in para 1 amended by reg 2(5) of SI 2016 No.1262 as from 15 January 2017, in relation to schemes made for financial years starting on or after 1 April 2017.

Noter-up

pp1112-15 **The Council Tax Reduction Schemes (Prescribed Requirements) (England) Regulations 2012 Sch 4 – Sums disregarded from applicant's earnings**
Para 5(1)(d)(ii) amended by Sch 1 para 8(4) of SI 2017 No.204 as from 3 April 2017, subject to transitional and savings provisions in Sch 2 paras 1–7.

pp1161-89 **The Council Tax Reduction Schemes and Prescribed Requirements (Wales) Regulations 2013 Sch 1 – Determining eligibility for a reduction under an authority's scheme, amount of reduction and calculation of income and capital: pensioners**
Amounts in para 3(1)(a) and (b) and (2)(a)–(c) amended by reg 3(a), the introductory words of para 11(1) amended and paras 11(3A) and (4A) inserted by reg 3(b), para 13(5)(a) amended by reg 3(c), para 22(1)(b) amended by reg 3(d), and para 24(1)(b) amended by reg 3(e) of SI 2017 No.46 (W.20) as from 19 January 2017, for schemes made for a financial year starting on or after 1 April 2017.

[p1161: In the General Note to Sch 1 para 1 at the end of the Note after "commentary", add:]

but note that council tax reduction schemes for pensioners should not place a restriction on the number of children for whom you can receive an amount under Sch 2 para 2 (ie, the so called 'two-child limit', which in some circumstances applies to HB, does not apply to CTR for pensioners).

[p1164: After the paragraph numbered (3) in the General Note to Sch 1 para 3, insert:]

(4) In respect of council tax reduction for pensioners in Wales, the amounts deducted for non-dependants are not the same as the amounts deducted in Scotland and England.

pp1189-93 **The Council Tax Reduction Schemes and Prescribed Requirements (Wales) Regulations 2013 Sch 2 – Applicable amounts: pensioners**
Amounts in column (2) of the table in para 1 amended by reg 4(a), para 6(2)(a)(iii) and the closing words of sub-para (b) and sub-paras (7)(d) and (8)(a) and (b) amended by reg 4(b), and sub-para (1)(b)(i) and (ii) in the table in para 12 and the amounts in that table amended by reg 4(c) of SI 2017 No.46 (W.20) as from 19 January 2017, for schemes made for a financial year starting on or after 1 April 2017.

[p1189: In the General Note to Sch 2 in the first sentence, delete ", but note that personal allowances for CTR in Wales for people aged 65 and over are higher than the equivalent amounts used to calculate HB entitlement for people subject to the HB(SPC) Regs and to calculate CTR for pensioners in England or Scotland".]

pp1204-27 **The Council Tax Reduction Schemes and Prescribed Requirements (Wales) Regulations 2013 Sch 6 – Determining eligibility for a reduction under an authority's scheme, amount of reduction and calculation of income and capital: persons who are not pensioners**
Amounts in para 5(1)(a) and (b) and (2)(a)–(c) amended by reg 5(a), para 10(2)(a) amended by reg 5(b), para 10A inserted by reg 5(c), para 15(6)(a) amended by reg 5(d), para 19(1)(a) amended by reg 5(e), 23(b) amended by reg 5(f), and para 25(1)(b) amended by reg 5(g), of SI 2017 No.46 (W.20) as from 19 January 2017, for schemes made for a financial year starting on or after 1 April 2017.

pp1227-37 **The Council Tax Reduction Schemes and Prescribed Requirements (Wales) Regulations 2013 Sch 7 – Applicable amounts: persons who are not pensioners**
Amounts in column (2) of the table in para 1 amended by reg 6(a), para 11(2)(a)(iii) and the closing words of sub-para (b) and sub-paras (5)(b), (6) and (7) amended by reg 6(b), sub-para (2)(b)(i) and (ii) in the table in para 17 and the amounts in that table amended by reg 6(c), the amount in para 23 amended by reg 6(d), and the amount in para 24 amended by reg 6(e), of SI 2017 No.46 (W.20) as from 19 January 2017, for schemes made for a financial year starting on or after 1 April 2017.

Noter-up

pp1292-94   The Council Tax Reduction Schemes (Default Scheme) (Wales) Regulations 2013 Sch para 28 – Non-dependant deductions: pensioners and persons who are not pensioners

Amounts in para (1)(a) and (b) and (2)(a)–(c) amended by reg 8 of SI 2017 No.46 (W.20) as from 19 January 2017, for schemes made for a financial year starting on or after 1 April 2017.

p1298   The Council Tax Reduction Schemes (Default Scheme) (Wales) Regulations 2013 Sch para 37 – Calculation of weekly income: pensioners

The introductory words of sub-para (1) amended, and sub-paras (3A) and (4A) inserted, by reg 9 of SI 2017 No.46 (W.20) as from 19 January 2017, for schemes made for a financial year starting on or after 1 April 2017.

pp1299-1300   The Council Tax Reduction Schemes (Default Scheme) (Wales) Regulations 2013 Sch para 39 – Calculation of net earnings of employed earners: pensioners

Sub-para (5)(a) amended by reg 10 of SI 2017 No.46 (W.20) as from 19 January 2017, for schemes made for a financial year starting on or after 1 April 2017.

pp1302-03   The Council Tax Reduction Schemes (Default Scheme) (Wales) Regulations 2013 Sch para 44 – Average weekly earnings of employed earners: persons who are not pensioners

Sub-para (2)(a) amended by reg 11, and para 44A inserted by reg 12, of SI 2017 No.46 (W.20) as from 19 January 2017, for schemes made for a financial year starting on or after 1 April 2017.

pp1304-05   The Council Tax Reduction Schemes (Default Scheme) (Wales) Regulations 2013 Sch para 49 – Calculation of net earnings of employed earners: persons who are not pensioners

Sub-para (6)(a) amended by reg 13 of SI 2017 No.46 (W.20) as from 19 January 2017, for schemes made for a financial year starting on or after 1 April 2017.

pp1307-08   The Council Tax Reduction Schemes (Default Scheme) (Wales) Regulations 2013 Sch para 53 – Notional income: persons who are not pensioners

Sub-para (10)(a) amended by reg 14 of SI 2017 No.46 (W.20) as from 19 January 2017, for schemes made for a financial year starting on or after 1 April 2017.

pp1312-13   The Council Tax Reduction Schemes (Default Scheme) (Wales) Regulations 2013 Sch para 57 – Disregard of changes in tax, contributions etc

Sub-para (a) amended by reg 15 of SI 2017 No.46 (W.20) as from 19 January 2017, for schemes made for a financial year starting on or after 1 April 2017.

pp1314-15   The Council Tax Reduction Schemes (Default Scheme) (Wales) Regulations 2013 Sch para 59 – Calculation of deduction of tax and contributions of self-employed earners

Sub-para (1)(b) amended by reg 16 of SI 2017 No.46 (W.20) as from 19 January 2017, for schemes made for a financial year starting on or after 1 April 2017.

pp1343-47   The Council Tax Reduction Schemes (Default Scheme) (Wales) Regulations 2013 Sch Sch 2 – Applicable amounts: pensioners

Amounts in column (2) of the table in para 1 amended by reg 17(a), para 6(2)(a)(iii) and the closing words of sub-para (b) and sub-paras (7)(d) and (8)(a) and (b) amended by reg 17(b), and sub-para (1)(b)(i) and (ii) in the table in para 12 and the amounts in that table amended by reg 17(c) of SI 2017 No.46 (W.20) as from 19 January 2017, for schemes made for a financial year starting on or after 1 April 2017.

pp1347-56   The Council Tax Reduction Schemes (Default Scheme) (Wales) Regulations 2013 Sch Sch 3 – Applicable amounts: persons who are not pensioners

Amounts in column (2) of the table in para 1 amended by reg 18(a), para 11(2)(a)(iii) and the closing words of sub-para (b) and sub-paras (5)(b), (6) and (7) amended by reg 18(b), and sub-

Noter-up

para (2)(b)(i) and (ii) in the table in para 17 and the amounts in that table amended by reg 18(c), the amount in para 23 amended by reg 18(d), and the amount in para 24 amended by reg 18(e), of SI 2017 No.46 (W.20) as from 19 January 2017, for schemes made for a financial year starting on or after 1 April 2017.

pp1391-1401 **The Council Tax Reduction (Scotland) Regulations 2012 reg 2 – Interpretation**
Definition of "infected blood payment scheme" inserted by reg 3 of SSI 2017 No.41 as from 1 April 2017.

pp1409-13 **The Council Tax Reduction (Scotland) Regulations 2012 reg 14 – Conditions of entitlement to council tax reduction**
The introductory words of para (1) amended, and para (3A) inserted, by reg 3 of SSI 2016 No.253 as from 1 April 2017.

[p1410: In the General Note, in the first paragraph replace "will be" with "have been", in the second paragraph replace "will be" with "has been" and replace the final sentence with:]

The amending regulations have been included in the supplement to this book, published in 2017.

[p1411: In the analysis, in the first paragraph, after "Reg 14" delete "sets" and replace with ", together with regulation 14A, set" and replace "it is" with "both regulation 14 and 14A are".]

[p1411: Under the heading "Subsections (1) and (3) to (7): Conditions of entitlement" immediately insert "Under reg 14," and after "para (3)" insert "and (3A)".]

[p1411: Under the heading "The general conditions" after the paragraph numbered (3) insert:]

(4) The amount of CTR to which an applicant is entitled under reg 14 must be equal to or more than the CTR s/he would be entitled to under reg 14A (if it is less, reg 14A determines entitlement): para (3A). Note that reg 14A can only apply if the dwelling in which the applicant resides is in council tax band E, F, G or H (see the General Note, above).

[p1411: Under the heading "Main CTR" in the first sentence, after "main CTR" insert "under reg 14".]

[p1412: Under the heading "Paras (8) and (9): Amount of CTR", replace the text with:]

The amount of CTR to which an applicant is entitled under reg 14 is either that calculated under para (8)(a) or (b) (main CTR) or that calculated under para 8(c) (alternative maximum CTR), whichever is higher.

An applicant who has no income, or whose income is equal to or less than her/his applicable amount, is entitled to the maximum CTR: para (8)(a). For how maximum CTR is calculated, see reg 66.

If the applicant's income is more than her/his applicable amount, entitlement to main CTR is calculated by deducting the percentage of the difference between the applicant's income and applicable amount from the maximum CTR: para 8(b).

If an applicant is entitled to alternative maximum CTR the amount is calculated in accordance with reg 78 and Sch 2: para (6) and para 8(c).

If an applicant qualifies for both main CTR and alternative maximum CTR, s/he is awarded the higher amount of the two, commonly referred to by local authorities as the "best buy": para (9).

From 1 April 2017, if the applicant's sole or main residence is in a dwelling in the council tax band E, F, G or H, a further calculation is done. This is the calculation of entitlement under reg 14A. If the applicant's entitlement under regulation 14 is equal to or higher than her/his entitlement under reg 14A, s/he will be entitled to the amount calculated in accordance with reg 14(8) and (9). If entitlement under reg 14A is higher than that under reg 14 s/he will be entitled to the amount calculated in accordance with reg 14A: para (3A) and reg 14A(1)(b).

Noter-up

p1413   **The Council Tax Reduction (Scotland) Regulations 2012 reg 14A – Conditions of entitlement to council tax reduction – dwellings in bands E to H**
Reg 14A inserted by reg 4 of SSI 2016 No.253 as from 1 April 2017.

pp1419-20   **The Council Tax Reduction (Scotland) Regulations 2012 reg 21 – Applicable amount**

[p1420: In the General Note, at the end of the Note add:]

but note that there is no restriction on the number of children for whom you can receive an amount under Sch 1 para 3 (ie, the so called 'two-child limit', which in some circumstances applies to HB, does not apply to CTR).

p1420   **The Council Tax Reduction (Scotland) Regulations 2012 reg 22 – Applicable amount: polygamous marriages**

[p1420: In the General Note, at the end of the Note add:]

but note that there is no restriction on the number of children for whom you can receive an amount under Sch 1 para 3 (ie, the so called 'two-child limit', which in some circumstances applies to HB, does not apply to CTR).

p1421   **The Council Tax Reduction (Scotland) Regulations 2012 reg 23 – Persons who have an award of universal credit**
Para (1) amended and para (2A) substituted by reg 4 of SSI 2017 No.41 as from 1 April 2017.

pp1422-23   **The Council Tax Reduction (Scotland) Regulations 2012 reg 27 – Calculation of income on a weekly basis**
The introductory words of para (1) amended by reg 5 of SSI 2016 No.253 as from 1 April 2017.

pp1436-39   **The Council Tax Reduction (Scotland) Regulations 2012 reg 41 – Notional income**
Para (4)(a) amended by reg 5 of SSI 2017 No.41 as from 1 April 2017.

pp1439-40   **The Council Tax Reduction (Scotland) Regulations 2012 reg 45 – Income treated as capital**
Para (6) amended by reg 6 of SSI 2017 No.41 as from 1 April 2017.

pp1440-42   **The Council Tax Reduction (Scotland) Regulations 2012 reg 48 – Notional capital**
Para (4)(a) amended by reg 7 of SSI 2017 No.41 as from 1 April 2017.

pp1452-53   **The Council Tax Reduction (Scotland) Regulations 2012 reg 66 – Maximum council tax reduction**
The introductory words of para (1) amended, paras (1A) and (1B) inserted, and para (2) amended by reg 6 of SSI 2016 No.253 as from 1 April 2017.

[p1453: In the General Note, in the first paragraph, replace "will be" with "have been" and in the second paragraph, replace "will be" in both places they occur with "has been".]

pp1453-55   **The Council Tax Reduction (Scotland) Regulations 2012 reg 67 – Non-dependant deductions**
Amounts in paras (1)(a) and (b) and (2)(a)–(c) amended and para (9)(b) amended by reg 8 of SSI 2017 No.41 as from 1 April 2017.

pp1460-01   **The Council Tax Reduction (Scotland) Regulations 2012 reg 80 – Date on which entitlement is to begin**
Paras (1)(b) and(2)(c) amended by reg 7 of SSI 2016 No.253 as from 1 April 2017.

Noter-up

pp1465-66 The Council Tax Reduction (Scotland) Regulations 2012 reg 86 – Evidence and information

Para (3)(a)(ii) amended by reg 9 of SSI 2017 No.41 as from 1 April 2017.

pp1471-81 The Council Tax Reduction (Scotland) Regulations 2012 Sch 1 – Applicable amount

Amounts in the table in para 3 amended by reg 8 of SSI 2016 No.253 as from 1 April 2017.

Amounts in the table in para 17 amended by reg 10(a), and amount in para 24 amended by reg 10(b), of SSI 2017 No.41 as from 1 April 2017.

[p1472: In the General Note above para 1, in the final paragraph replace "is to be" with "has been" and delete the final sentence which begins "See the...".]

pp1481-82 The Council Tax Reduction (Scotland) Regulations 2012 Sch 2 – Amount of alternative maximum council tax reduction

Amounts in sub-para (b)(i) and (ii) of column (1) in the table in para 1 amended by reg 11(a), and para 2(b) amended by reg 11(b), of SSI 2017 No.41 as from 1 April 2017.

pp1485-93 The Council Tax Reduction (Scotland) Regulations 2012 Sch 4 – Sums to be disregarded in the calculation of income other than earnings

Para 41(1) and (7) amended by reg 12 of SSI 2017 No.41 as from 1 April 2017.

pp1493-00 The Council Tax Reduction (Scotland) Regulations 2012 Sch 5 – Capital to be disregarded

Para 38 amended by reg 13 of SSI 2017 No.41 as from 1 April 2017.

pp1505-14 The Council Tax Reduction (State Pension Credit) (Scotland) Regulations 2012 reg 2 – Interpretation

Definition of "infected blood payment scheme" inserted by reg 15 of SSI 2017 No.41 as from 1 April 2017.

pp1521-23 The Council Tax Reduction (State Pension Credit) (Scotland) Regulations 2012 reg 14 – Conditions of entitlement to council tax reduction

The introductory words of para (1) amended, and para (3A) inserted, by reg 10 of SSI 2016 No.253 as from 1 April 2017.

[p1522: In the General Note, in the first paragraph replace "will be" with "has been" and in the second paragraph replace "will be" with "has been".]

[p1523: In the General Note, in the final sentence replace "will be" with "have been".]

p1523 The Council Tax Reduction (State Pension Credit) (Scotland) Regulations 2012 reg 14A – Conditions of entitlement to council tax reduction – dwellings in bands E to H

Reg 14A inserted by reg 11 of SSI 2016 No.253 as from 1 April 2017.

p1532 The Council Tax Reduction (State Pension Credit) (Scotland) Regulations 2012 reg 28 – Calculation of income on a weekly basis

The introductory words of para (1) amended by reg 12 of SSI 2016 No.253 as from 1 April 2017.

pp1550-51 The Council Tax Reduction (State Pension Credit) (Scotland) Regulations 2012 reg 47 – Maximum council tax reduction

The introductory words of para (1) amended, and paras (1A) and (1B) inserted, and para (2) amended by reg 13 of SSI 2016 No.253 as from 1 April 2017.

[p1551: In the General Note, in the first paragraph replace "will be" with "have been" and in the second paragraph – in both places they occur – replace "will be" with "has been".]

Noter-up

pp1551-53 The Council Tax Reduction (State Pension Credit) (Scotland) Regulations 2012 reg 48 – Non-dependant deductions
Amounts in paras (1)(a) and (b) and (2)(a)–(c) amended and para (9)(b) amended by reg 16 of SSI 2017 No.41 as from 1 April 2017.

[p1551: In the General Note, in the first paragraph replace "will be" with "have been" and in the second paragraph – in both places they occur – replace "will be" with "has been".]

p1557 The Council Tax Reduction (State Pension Credit) (Scotland) Regulations 2012 reg 58 – Date on which entitlement begins
Paras (1)(b) and (2)(c) amended by reg 14 of SSI 2016 No.253 as from 1 April 2017.

p1563 The Council Tax Reduction (State Pension Credit) (Scotland) Regulations 2012 reg 66 – Evidence and information
Para (3)(a) amended by reg 17 of SSI 2017 No.41 as from 1 April 2017.

pp1569-73 The Council Tax Reduction (State Pension Credit) (Scotland) Regulations 2012 Sch 1 – Applicable amount
Amounts in column (2) of the table in para 2 amended by reg 18(a), and amounts in the table in para 13 amended by reg 18(b), of SSI 2017 No.41 as from 1 April 2017.

Amounts in column (2) of the table in para 3 amended by reg 15 of SSI 2016 No.253 as from 1 April 2017.

[p1569: In the General Note above para 1, in the final paragraph replace "will be" with "has been" and delete the final sentence which begins "See the…".]

pp1579-83 The Council Tax Reduction (State Pension Credit) (Scotland) Regulations 2012 Sch 4 – Capital disregards
Para 16(1)(a), (7) and (8) amended by reg 19 of SSI 2017 No.41 as from 1 April 2017.

pp1584-85 The Council Tax Reduction (State Pension Credit) (Scotland) Regulations 2012 Sch 5 – Amount of alternative maximum council tax reduction
Amounts in sub-paras (b)(i) and (ii) in column (1) in the table in para 1 amended by reg 20(a), and para 2(b) amended by reg 20(b), of SSI 2017 No.41 as from 1 April 2017.

pp1591-93 The Valuation Tribunal for England (Council Tax and Rating Appeals) (Procedure) Regulations 2009 reg 2 – Interpretation: definition of "appeal"
Definition of "NDR appeal" inserted, para (3)(d)(i) amended and paras (4) and (5) inserted by reg 4 by SI 2017 No.156 as from 1 April 2017, in relation to a local non-domestic rating list and a central non-domestic rating list compiled on or after 1 April 2017.

pp1593-94 The Valuation Tribunal for England (Council Tax and Rating Appeals) (Procedure) Regulations 2009 reg 6 – Appeal management powers
Paras (3)(c) and (d) amended and para (4) inserted by reg 6 by SI 2017 No.156 as from 1 April 2017, in relation to a local non-domestic rating list and a central non-domestic rating list compiled on or after 1 April 2017.

pp1597-98 The Valuation Tribunal for England (Council Tax and Rating Appeals) (Procedure) Regulations 2009 reg 17 – Evidence and submissions
Para (1) amended, para (1A) inserted, para (2) amended and para (4)(c) inserted by reg 8 by SI 2017 No.156 as from 1 April 2017, in relation to a local non-domestic rating list and a central non-domestic rating list compiled on or after 1 April 2017.

p1598 The Valuation Tribunal for England (Council Tax and Rating Appeals) (Procedure) Regulations 2009 reg 18 – Summoning of witnesses, and orders to answer questions or produce documents
Para (A1) inserted by reg 10 by SI 2017 No.156 as from 1 April 2017, in relation to a local non-domestic rating list and a central non-domestic rating list compiled on or after 1 April 2017.

Noter-up

pp1600-01 The Valuation Tribunal for England (Council Tax and Rating Appeals) (Procedure) Regulations 2009 reg 36 – Notice of decisions

Paras (3) and (4) inserted by SI 2017 No.156 as from 1 April 2017, in relation to a local non-domestic rating list and a central non-domestic rating list compiled on or after 1 April 2017.

p1590 The Valuation Tribunal for England (Council Tax and Rating Appeals) (Procedure) Regulations 2009 – General Note

[p1590: In the General Note in the paragraph which begins "For the purpose of these regulations…", delete "The Practice Statement Council Tax Reduction Appeals (VTE/PS/A11, paras 3–6) contains guidance for situations where the information provided is incomplete."]

[p1590: In the General Note, after the end of the final paragraph, add a new paragraph:]

Standard directions for council tax reduction appeals are contained in the Valuation Tribunal for England Consolidated Practice Statement 2017 (VTE CPS 2017), PS6, pp21–22.

pp1695-01 HB&CTB(CP) Regs Sch 3 para 4

[p1699: In the Analysis of sub-paragraphs (1)(b) and (10): Exempt accommodation, after the paragraph starting "In R(H) 2/07 … ", add a new paragraph:]

In *MMcF v Sefton BC (HB)* [2016] UKUT 403 (AAC), a support package for the claimant had been commissioned by the local authority and was provided by an organisation other than his landlord. His landlord also provided regular support. However, the local authority decided that the claimant did not live in "exempt accommodation", it said because support or supervision provided by a landlord must not duplicate functions and tasks already covered in a main support plan, and this was accepted by the First-tier Tribunal. Judge Brunner QC pointed out that there was nothing in the regulations to support this view. Following *R(H) 7/07*, she allowed the claimant's appeal. She said that duplication may be a useful evidential consideration to enable a local authority or tribunal to address the relevant legal issues, but it is not a legal hurdle in itself.

[p1699: In the Analysis of sub-paragraphs (1)(b) and (10): Exempt accommodation, after the first paragraph starting "where that body or a person acting … ", add a new paragraph:]

In *AG v South Ayrshire Council (HB)* [2017] UKUT 110 (AAC), the First-tier Tribunal had decided that the claimant's accommodation was not "exempt accommodation". It said that although his landlord was providing support that was more than minimal, the landlord was required to register under s59 of the Public Services Reform (Scotland) Act 2010, and because it had not done so, the services it provided were unlawfully provided. The Upper Tribunal allowed the appeal. The judge said that:

> "… a tribunal does not have an independent jurisdiction to determine whether or not a provider is complying with some other regulatory regime. The situation would be different if a court having jurisdiction had determined that *[the landlord]* could not lawfully provide care services. Then that would be a fact to be taken into account by the FtT in determining whether or not care services were being provided that fell within the definition of "care, support or supervision" under regulation 4(10). *[R v HBRB for Allerdale District Council ex p Doughty* [2000] COD 462 QBD] is an example. In that case the application for registration as a small residential home was rejected by the Registered Homes Tribunal. The fact that registration had been rejected by the regulator meant that care services could not be lawfully provided. The Housing Board then made their decision on the basis of the fact that the proper regulatory body had refused registration and so care could not be provided."

pp1794-5 The Welfare Reform Act 2012 (Commencement No.23 and Transitional and Transitory provisions) Order 2015 reg 7 – Transitional provisions: claims for housing benefit, income support or a tax credit

Para (2) amended by reg 4 of SI 2017 No.376 as from 6 April 2017.

PART II:

SECONDARY LEGISLATION

The Council Tax Reduction (Scotland) Amendment (No.2) Regulations 2016

(2016 No.253)

Made 6th September 2016
Laid before the Scottish Parliament 7th September 2016
Coming into force 1st April 2017

The Scottish Ministers make the following Regulations in exercise of the powers conferred by sections 80 and 113(1) and (2) and paragraph 1 of schedule 2 of the Local Government Finance Act 1992 and all other powers enabling them to do so.

Citation and commencement
1. These Regulations may be cited as the Council Tax Reduction (Scotland) Amendment (No. 2) Regulations 2016 and come into force on 1st April 2017.

Amendment of the Council Tax Reduction (Scotland) Regulations 2012
2. The Council Tax Reduction (Scotland) Regulations 2012 are amended as follows.

Amendment of the Council Tax Reduction (Scotland) Regulations 2012
3. In regulation 14 (conditions of entitlement to council tax reduction)–
(a) in paragraph (1)–
    (i) after "reduction", insert "under this regulation"; and
    (ii) for "paragraph (3)", substitute "paragraphs (3) and (3A)"; and
(b) after paragraph (3), insert–

"(3A) The condition referred to in paragraph (1) is that the amount of council tax reduction calculated under this regulation is not less than the amount of council tax reduction calculated under regulation 14A.".

Amendment of the Council Tax Reduction (Scotland) Regulations 2012
4. After regulation 14, insert–

"Conditions of entitlement to council tax reduction – dwellings in bands E to H
14A.–(1) A person who is liable to pay council tax under section 75 of the Act ("relevant person") is entitled to council tax reduction under this regulation in respect of a day if–
(a) the conditions set out in paragraph (3) to (5) are satisfied; and
(b) the amount of council tax reduction calculated under this regulation is greater than the amount of council tax reduction calculated under regulation 14.
(2) A relevant person is not entitled to council tax reduction in respect of any day before the day on which that person's entitlement to council tax reduction commences in accordance with regulation 80 (date on which entitlement is to begin).
(3) The conditions referred to in paragraph (1)(a) are that the relevant person–
(a) is for the day liable to pay council tax in respect of a dwelling in valuation band E, F, G or H in which that person resides as their sole or main residence;
(b) is not a person to whom regulation 15 (persons not entitled to council tax reduction: absentees), 16 (persons not entitled to council tax reduction: persons treated as not being in Great Britain), 19 (persons not entitled to council tax reduction: persons subject to immigration control) or 20 (persons not entitled to council tax reduction: students) applies; and
(c) makes an application for council tax reduction in accordance with Part 10 (applications).

(4) The condition referred to in paragraph (1)(a) is that there is an appropriate maximum council tax reduction in the case of the relevant person.
(5) The condition referred to in paragraph (1)(a) is that–
(a) the day falls within a week in respect of which–
 (i) the relevant person has no income; or
 (ii) the relevant person's income does not exceed–
  (aa) £321, in the case of a person to whom paragraph (6) applies;
  (bb) £479, in any other case; or
(b) neither sub-paragraph (a)(i) or (ii) applies to the relevant person but amount A exceeds amount B where–
 (i) amount A is the appropriate maximum council tax reduction in the relevant person's case; and
 (ii) amount B is 2 6/7 per cent of the difference between the person's income in respect of the week in which the day falls and the amount stated in sub-paragraph (a)(ii)(aa) or (bb) (as the case may be).
(6) This paragraph applies to a person who–
(a) is not a member of a couple or of a polygamous marriage; and
(b) is not responsible for a child or young person (within the meaning of regulation 10).
(7) Where a relevant person is entitled to council tax reduction in respect of a day, the amount to which the person is entitled is–
(a) if paragraph (5)(a) applies, the amount which is the appropriate maximum council tax reduction in that person's case;
(b) if paragraph (5)(b) applies, the amount found by deducting amount B from amount A, where "amount A" and "amount B" have the meanings given by that paragraph.".

Amendment of the Council Tax Reduction (Scotland) Regulations 2012
5. In paragraph (1) of regulation 27 (calculation of income on a weekly basis), after "14(5)" insert "or 14A(5)".

Amendment of the Council Tax Reduction (Scotland) Regulations 2012
6. In regulation 66 (maximum council tax reduction)–
(a) in paragraph (1), after "and (3)," insert "for the purposes of regulation 14";
(b) after paragraph (1), insert–

"(1A) Subject to paragraphs (2) and (3), for the purposes of regulation 14A the amount of a person's maximum council tax reduction in respect of a day for which the person is liable to pay council tax is 100% of the amount–

$$\frac{A - A/C}{B}$$

less any deductions in respect of non-dependants which fall to be made under regulation 67.
(1B) In paragraph (1A)–
(a) A and B have the same meanings as in paragraph (1); and
(b) C is–
 (i) 1.075 if the relevant dwelling is in valuation band E;
 (ii) 1.125 if the relevant dwelling is in valuation band F;
 (iii) 1.175 if the relevant dwelling is in valuation band G;
 (iv) 1.225 if the relevant dwelling is in valuation band H."; and
(c) in paragraph (2), after "paragraph (1)" insert "or (1A)".

Amendment of the Council Tax Reduction (Scotland) Regulations 2012
7. In regulation 80 (date on which entitlement is to begin)–
(a) in paragraph (1)(b), after "regulation 14" insert "or 14A"; and
(b) in paragraph (2)(c), after "regulation 14" insert "or 14A".

(SI 2016 No.253, reg 11)

Amendment of the Council Tax Reduction (Scotland) Regulations 2012
8. In schedule 1 (applicable amount), in paragraph 3 for "£66.90" (in both places where it occurs) substitute "£83.63".

Amendment of the Council Tax Reduction (State Pension Credit) (Scotland) Regulations 2012
9. The Council Tax Reduction (State Pension Credit) (Scotland) Regulations 2012 are amended as follows.

Amendment of the Council Tax Reduction (State Pension Credit) (Scotland) Regulations 2012
10. In regulation 14 (conditions of entitlement to council tax reduction)–
(a) in paragraph (1)–
    (i) after "reduction", insert "under this regulation"; and
    (ii) for "paragraph (3)", substitute "paragraphs (3) and (3A)"; and
(b) after paragraph (3), insert–

"(3A) The condition referred to in paragraph (1) is that the amount of council tax reduction calculated under this regulation is not less than the amount of council tax reduction calculated under regulation 14A.".

Amendment of the Council Tax Reduction (State Pension Credit) (Scotland) Regulations 2012
11. After regulation 14, insert–

"Conditions of entitlement to council tax reduction – dwellings in bands E to H
14A.–(1) A person who is liable to pay council tax under section 75 of the Act ("relevant person") is entitled to council tax reduction under this regulation in respect of a day if–
(a) the conditions set out in paragraph (3) to (5) are satisfied; and
(b) the amount of council tax reduction calculated under this regulation is greater than the amount of council tax reduction calculated under regulation 14.
(2) A relevant person is not entitled to council tax reduction in respect of any day before the day on which that person's entitlement to council tax reduction commences in accordance with regulation 58 (date on which entitlement begins).
(3) The conditions referred to in paragraph (1)(a) are that the relevant person–
(a) is for the day liable to pay council tax in respect of a dwelling in valuation band E, F, G or H in which that person resides as their sole or main residence;
(b) is not a person to whom regulation 15 (persons not entitled to council tax reduction: absentees), 16 (persons not entitled to council tax reduction: persons treated as not being in Great Britain) or 19 (persons not entitled to council tax reduction: persons subject to immigration control) applies; and
(c) makes an application for council tax reduction in accordance with Part 9 (applications).
(4) The condition referred to in paragraph (1)(a) is that there is an appropriate maximum council tax reduction in the case of the relevant person.
(5) The condition referred to in paragraph (1)(a) is that–
(a) the day falls within a week in respect of which–
    (i) the relevant person has no income; or
    (ii) the relevant person's income does not exceed–
        (aa) £321, in the case of a person to whom paragraph (6) applies;
        (bb) £479, in any other case; or
(b) neither sub-paragraph (a)(i) or (ii) applies to the relevant person but amount A exceeds amount B where–
    (i) amount A is the appropriate maximum council tax reduction in the relevant person's case; and

(ii) amount B is 2 6/7 per cent of the difference between the person's income in respect of the week in which the day falls and the amount stated in sub-paragraph (a)(ii)(aa) or (bb) (as the case may be).

(6) This paragraph applies to a person who–
 (a) is not a member of a couple or of a polygamous marriage; and
 (b) is not responsible for a child or young person (within the meaning of regulation 10).

(7) Where a relevant person is entitled to council tax reduction in respect of a day, the amount to which the person is entitled is–
 (a) if paragraph (5)(a) applies, the amount which is the appropriate maximum council tax reduction in that person's case;
 (b) if paragraph (5)(b) applies, the amount found by deducting amount B from amount A, where "amount A" and "amount B" have the meanings given by that paragraph.".

Amendment of the Council Tax Reduction (State Pension Credit) (Scotland) Regulations 2012

12. In paragraph (1) of regulation 28 (calculation of income on a weekly basis), after "14(5)" insert "or 14A(5)".

Amendment of the Council Tax Reduction (State Pension Credit) (Scotland) Regulations 2012

13. In regulation 47 (maximum council tax reduction)–
 (a) in paragraph (1), after "and (3)," insert "for the purposes of regulation 14";
 (b) after paragraph (1), insert–

"(1A) Subject to paragraphs (2) and (3), for the purposes of regulation 14A the amount of a person's maximum council tax reduction in respect of a day for which the person is liable to pay council tax is 100% of the amount–
less any deductions in respect of non-dependants which fall to be made under regulation 48.

(1B) In paragraph (1A)–
 (a) A and B have the same meanings as in paragraph (1); and
 (b) C is–
  (i) 1.075 if the relevant dwelling is in valuation band E;
  (ii) 1.125 if the relevant dwelling is in valuation band F;
  (iii) 1.175 if the relevant dwelling is in valuation band G;
  (iv) 1.225 if the relevant dwelling is in valuation band H."; and

 (c) in paragraph (2), after "paragraph (1)" insert "or (1A)".

Amendment of the Council Tax Reduction (State Pension Credit) (Scotland) Regulations 2012

14. In regulation 58 (date on which entitlement begins)–
 (a) in paragraph (1)(b), after "regulation 14" insert "or 14A"; and
 (b) in paragraph (2)(c), after "regulation 14" insert "or 14A".

Amendment of the Council Tax Reduction (State Pension Credit) (Scotland) Regulations 2012

15. In schedule 1 (applicable amount), in paragraph 3 for "£66.90" (in both places where it occurs) substitute "£83.63".

The Rent Officers (Housing Benefit and Universal Credit Functions) (Local Housing Allowance Amendments) Order 2016

(2016 No.1179)

Made	6th December 2016
Laid before Parliament	12th December 2016
Coming into force	23rd January 2017

The Secretary of State makes the following Order in exercise of the powers conferred by sections 122(1) and (6) of the Housing Act 1996.

Citation and commencement
1. This Order may be cited as the Rent Officers (Housing Benefit and Universal Credit Functions) (Local Housing Allowance Amendments) Order 2016 and comes into force on 23rd January 2017.

Amendment of the Rent Officers (Housing Benefit Functions) Order 1997
2.–(1) The Rent Officers (Housing Benefit Functions) Order 1997(2) is amended as follows.
(2) In article 4B, after paragraph (1A) (broad rental market area determinations)(3), insert–

"(1B) The power in paragraph (1A) is not limited by paragraph 2(2A) or (2B) of Schedule 3B.".

(3) In Schedule 3B (broad rental market determinations and local housing allowance determinations)(4)–
(a) in paragraph 2 (local housing allowance determinations)–
   (i) before sub-paragraph (3) insert–

"(2A) For a broad rental market area not listed in column 1 of the table in paragraph 5A, the local housing allowance for any category of dwelling is the lower of the amounts set out in sub-paragraph (3)(a) and (b).
(2B) For a broad rental market area listed in column 1 of the table in paragraph 5A, the local housing allowance–
(a) for a category of dwelling listed in the corresponding entry in column 2 of that table, is the lower of the amounts set out in sub-paragraph (3A)(a) and (b);
(b) for a category of dwelling not so listed, is the lower of the amounts set out in sub-paragraph (3)(a) and (b).";

   (ii) in sub-paragraph (3)–
      (aa) for the words before paragraph (a) substitute "The amounts referred to in sub-paragraphs (2A) and (2B)(b) are–";
      (bb) at the end of paragraph (a), for "or" substitute "and";
      (cc) in paragraph (b), omit ", where that rent is lower than the allowance referred to in paragraph (a)";
   (iii) after sub-paragraph (3) insert–

"(3A) The amounts referred to in sub-paragraph (2B)(a) are–
(a) the local housing allowance determined for that category of dwelling on 30th January 2015 (or, where the determination is amended under article 7A(4) (errors), the allowance provided for in the amended determination), plus 3%; and
(b) the maximum local housing allowance listed in column 2 of the following table for the category of dwelling–

1. Category of dwelling as defined in the following paragraphs of this Schedule	2. Maximum local housing allowance for that category of dwelling
paragraph 1(1)(a) (one bedroom, shared accommodation)	£260.64
paragraph 1(1)(b) (one bedroom, exclusive use)	£260.64
paragraph 1(1)(c) (two bedrooms)	£302.33
paragraph 1(1)(d) (three bedrooms)	£354.46
paragraph 1(1)(e) (four bedrooms)	£417.02"

(b) after paragraph 5 insert–

"5A. The table referred to in paragraph 2(2A) and (2B) is as follows–

1. Broad rental market area	2. Category of dwelling as defined in the following paragraphs of this Schedule
Aylesbury	paragraph 1(1)(b) (one bedroom, exclusive use)
Aylesbury	paragraph 1(1)(c) (two bedrooms)
Barrow-in-Furness	paragraph 1(1)(a) (one bedroom, shared accommodation)
Bedford	paragraph 1(1)(d) (three bedrooms)
Bolton and Bury	paragraph 1(1)(a) (one bedroom, shared accommodation)
Bristol	paragraph 1(1)(b) (one bedroom, exclusive use)
Bristol	paragraph 1(1)(d) (three bedrooms)
Bury St. Edmunds	paragraph 1(1)(a) (one bedroom, shared accommodation)
Cambridge	paragraph 1(1)(c) (two bedrooms)
Cambridge	paragraph 1(1)(e) (four bedrooms)
Central London	paragraph 1(1)(a) (one bedroom, shared accommodation)
Central Norfolk and Norwich	paragraph 1(1)(a) (one bedroom, shared accommodation)
Chilterns	paragraph 1(1)(c) (two bedrooms)
Flintshire	paragraph 1(1)(a) (one bedroom, shared accommodation)
Harlow and Stortford	paragraph 1(1)(a) (one bedroom, shared accommodation)
Inner North London	paragraph 1(1)(a) (one bedroom, shared accommodation)
Kings Lynn	paragraph 1(1)(a) (one bedroom, shared accommodation)
Luton	paragraph 1(1)(b) (one bedroom, exclusive use)
Luton	paragraph 1(1)(c) (two bedrooms)
Luton	paragraph 1(1)(d) (three bedrooms)
Luton	paragraph 1(1)(e) (four bedrooms)
Milton Keynes	paragraph 1(1)(d) (three bedrooms)
Milton Keynes	paragraph 1(1)(e) (four bedrooms)
Neath Port Talbot	paragraph 1(1)(a) (one bedroom, shared accommodation)
North West Kent	paragraph 1(1)(e) (four bedrooms)
North West London	paragraph 1(1)(b) (one bedroom, exclusive use)
Outer East London	paragraph 1(1)(a) (one bedroom, shared accommodation)
Outer East London	paragraph 1(1)(e) (four bedrooms)
Outer South London	paragraph 1(1)(b) (one bedroom, exclusive use)
Outer South London	paragraph 1(1)(c) (two bedrooms)
Outer South West London	paragraph 1(1)(a) (one bedroom, shared accommodation)

Outer West London	paragraph 1(1)(c) (two bedrooms)
Pembrokeshire	paragraph 1(1)(a) (one bedroom, shared accommodation)
Solihull	paragraph 1(1)(a) (one bedroom, shared accommodation)
South West Essex	paragraph 1(1)(a) (one bedroom, shared accommodation)
South West Herts	paragraph 1(1)(d) (three bedrooms)
Southend	paragraph 1(1)(a) (one bedroom, shared accommodation)
Southern Greater Manchester	paragraph 1(1)(a) (one bedroom, shared accommodation)
Stevenage & North Herts	paragraph 1(1)(b) (one bedroom, exclusive use)
Stevenage & North Herts	paragraph 1(1)(d) (three bedrooms)
Stevenage & North Herts	paragraph 1(1)(e) (four bedrooms)
Sunderland	paragraph 1(1)(a) (one bedroom, shared accommodation)
Swindon	paragraph 1(1)(a) (one bedroom, shared accommodation)
Swindon	paragraph 1(1)(b) (one bedroom, exclusive use)
Vale of Glamorgan	paragraph 1(1)(a) (one bedroom, shared accommodation)
Walton	paragraph 1(1)(a) (one bedroom, shared accommodation)
Warwickshire South	paragraph 1(1)(a) (one bedroom, shared accommodation)"

Amendment of the Rent Officers (Housing Benefit Functions) (Scotland) Order 1997

3.–(1) The Rent Officers (Housing Benefit Functions) (Scotland) Order 1997(1) is amended as follows.

(2) In article 4B, after paragraph (1A) (broad rental market area determinations)(2), insert–

"(1B) The power in paragraph (1A) is not limited by paragraph 2(2A) or (2B) of Schedule 3B.".

(3) In paragraph 2 of Schedule 3B (local housing allowance determinations)(3)–
(a) before sub-paragraph (3) insert–

"(2A) For all broad rental market areas other than Lothian, the local housing allowance for any category of dwelling is the lower of the amounts set out in sub-paragraph (3)(a) and (b).
(2B) For the Lothian broad rental market area, the local housing allowance–
(a) for the category of dwelling defined in paragraph 1(1)(b) of this Schedule (one bedroom, exclusive use), is the lower of the amounts set out in sub-paragraph (3A)(a) and (b);
(b) for all other categories of dwelling, is the lower of the amounts set out in sub-paragraph (3)(a) and (b).";

(b) in sub-paragraph (3)–
   (i) for the words before paragraph (a) substitute "The amounts referred to in sub-paragraphs (2A) and (2B)(b) are–";
   (ii) at the end of paragraph (a), for "or" substitute "and";
   (iii) in paragraph (b), omit ", where that rent is lower than the allowance referred to in paragraph (a)";

(c) after sub-paragraph (3) insert–

"(3A) The amounts referred to in (2B)(a) are–
(a) the local housing allowance determined for that category of dwelling on 30th January 2015 (or, where the determination is amended under article 7A(4) (errors), the allowance provided for in the amended determination), plus 3%; and
(b) £260.64.".

The Council Tax Reduction Schemes (Prescribed Requirements) (England) (Amendment) Regulations 2016
(2016 No.1262)

Made	21st December 2016
Laid before Parliament	22nd December 2016
Coming into force	15th January 2017

The Secretary of State makes the following Regulations in exercise of the powers conferred by section 113(1) and (2) of, and paragraph 2 of Schedule 1A to, the Local Government Finance Act 1992:

Citation, commencement and application

1.–(1) These Regulations may be cited as the Council Tax Reduction Schemes (Prescribed Requirements) (England) (Amendment) Regulations 2016 and come into force on 15th January 2017.

(2) These Regulations apply in relation to council tax reduction schemes made by billing authorities for financial years beginning on or after 1st April 2017.

Amendment of the Council Tax Reduction Schemes (Prescribed Requirements) (England) Regulations 2012

2.–(1) The Council Tax Reduction Schemes (Prescribed Requirements) (England) Regulations 2012(1) are amended as follows.

(2) In regulation 2(1) (interpretation) after the definition of "savings credit" insert–

""Scottish basic rate" means the rate of income tax of that name calculated in accordance with section 6A of the Income Tax Act 2007;
"Scottish taxpayer" has the same meaning as in Chapter 2 of Part 4A of the Scotland Act 1998;".

(3) In Schedule 1 (pensioners: matters that must be included in an authority's scheme)–
  (a) in paragraph 5 (periods of absence from a dwelling)–
     (i) in sub-paragraph (2)(a) after "residential accommodation" insert "in Great Britain";
     (ii) in sub-paragraph (2)(b) for "a period of absence" substitute "subject to sub-paragraph (2B), a period of absence within Great Britain";
     (iii) at the end of sub-paragraph (2)(b) omit "and";
     (iv) in sub-paragraph (2)(c) for "a period of absence" substitute "subject to sub-paragraph (2D), a period of absence within Great Britain";
     (v) at the end of sub-paragraph (2)(c) for the full stop substitute "; and";
     (vi) after sub-paragraph (2)(c) insert–

"(d) subject to sub-paragraphs (2F), (3C), (3E) and (3G) and where sub-paragraph (2E) applies, a period of absence outside Great Britain not exceeding 4 weeks, beginning with the first day of that absence from Great Britain where and for so long as–
  (i) the person intends to return to the dwelling;
  (ii) the part of the dwelling in which he usually resides is not let or sub-let; and
  (iii) the period of absence from Great Britain is unlikely to exceed 4 weeks.";

     (vii) after sub-paragraph (2) insert–

"(2A) The period of 13 weeks referred to in sub-paragraph (2)(b) shall run or continue to run during any period of absence from Great Britain.

(2B) Where—
(a) a person returns to Great Britain after a period of absence from Great Britain (period A);
(b) that person has been absent from the dwelling, including any absence within Great Britain, for less than 13 weeks beginning with the first day of absence from that dwelling; and
(c) at the outset of, or during, period A, period A ceased to be treated as a period of temporary absence,

then any day that follows period A and precedes the person's return to the dwelling, shall not be treated as a period of temporary absence under sub-paragraph (2)(b).

(2C) The period of 52 weeks referred to in sub-paragraph (2)(c) shall run or continue to run during any period of absence from Great Britain.

(2D) Where—
(a) a person returns to Great Britain after a period of absence from Great Britain (period A);
(b) that person has been absent from the dwelling, including any absence within Great Britain, for less than 52 weeks beginning with the first day of absence from that dwelling; and
(c) at the outset of, or during, period A, period A ceased to be treated as a period of temporary absence,

then, any day that follows period A and precedes the person's return to the dwelling, shall not be treated as a period of temporary absence under sub-paragraph (2)(c).

(2E) This sub-paragraph applies where—
(a) a person is temporarily absent from Great Britain;
(b) immediately before that period of absence from Great Britain, the person was not absent from the dwelling.

(2F) If the temporary absence referred to in sub-paragraph (2)(d) is in connection with the death of—
(a) the person's partner or a child or young person for whom the person or the person's partner is responsible;
(b) the person's close relative;
(c) the close relative of the person's partner; or
(d) the close relative of a child or young person for whom the person or the person's partner is responsible,

then the period of 4 weeks in the opening words of sub-paragraph (2)(d) may be extended by up to 4 further weeks if the relevant authority considers it unreasonable to expect the person to return to Great Britain within the first 4 weeks (and the reference in sub-paragraph (iii) of that paragraph to a period of 4 weeks shall, where the period is extended, be taken as referring to the period as so extended).";

(viii) in sub-paragraph (3)—
(aa) for paragraph (a) substitute—

"(a) is a person to whom sub-paragraph (3A) applies;"

(bb) in paragraph (c) omit ", in the United Kingdom or elsewhere,";
(cc) in paragraph (d) omit ", in the United Kingdom or elsewhere,";
(dd) in paragraph (e) omit "residing in the United Kingdom or elsewhere";
(ee) in paragraph (g) omit ", in the United Kingdom or elsewhere,";
(ix) after sub-paragraph (3) insert—

"(3A) This sub-paragraph applies to a person ("P") who is—
(a) detained in custody on remand pending trial;
(b) detained pending sentence upon conviction; or
(c) as a condition of bail required to reside—
(i) in a dwelling, other than a dwelling P occupies as P's home; or

(ii) in premises approved under section 13 of the Offender Management Act 2007,
and who is not also detained in custody following sentence upon conviction.
(3B) This sub-paragraph applies where–
(a) a person is temporarily absent from Great Britain;
(b) the person is a member of Her Majesty's forces posted overseas, a mariner or a continental shelf worker;
(c) immediately before that period of absence from Great Britain, the person was not absent from the dwelling.
(3C) Where sub-paragraph (3B) applies, a period of absence from Great Britain not exceeding 26 weeks, beginning with the first day of absence from Great Britain, shall be treated as a period of temporary absence where and for so long as–
(a) the person intends to return to the dwelling;
(b) the part of the dwelling in which he usually resided is not let or sub-let;
(c) the period of absence from Great Britain is unlikely to exceed 26 weeks.
(3D) This sub-paragraph applies where–
(a) a person is temporarily absent from Great Britain;
(b) the person is a person described in any of paragraphs (b), (c), (g) or (j) of sub-paragraph (3);
(c) immediately before that period of absence from Great Britain, the person was not absent from the dwelling.
(3E) Where sub-paragraph (3D) applies, a period of absence from Great Britain not exceeding 26 weeks, beginning with the first day of absence from Great Britain, shall be treated as a period of temporary absence where and for so long as–
(a) the person intends to return to the dwelling;
(b) the part of the dwelling in which he usually resided is not let or sub-let;
(c) the period of absence is unlikely to exceed 26 weeks, or in exceptional circumstances, is unlikely substantially to exceed that period.
(3F) This sub-paragraph applies where–
(a) a person is temporarily absent from Great Britain;
(b) the person is a person described in any of paragraphs (a), (d), (e), (f), (h) or (i) of sub-paragraph (3);
(c) immediately before that period of absence from Great Britain, the person was not absent from the dwelling.
(3G) Where sub-paragraph (3F) applies, a period of absence from Great Britain not exceeding 4 weeks, beginning with the first day of absence from Great Britain, shall be treated as a period of temporary absence where and for so long as–
(a) the person intends to return to the dwelling;
(b) the part of the dwelling in which he usually resided is not let or sub-let;
(c) the period of absence is unlikely to exceed 4 weeks, or in exceptional circumstances, is unlikely substantially to exceed that period.";

(x) in sub-paragraph (6)–
(aa) before the definition of "medically approved" insert–

""continental shelf worker" means a person who is employed, whether under a contract of service or not, in a designated area or a prescribed area in connection with any of the activities mentioned in section 11(2) of the Petroleum Act 1998;
"designated area" means any area which may from time to time be designated by Order in Council under the Continental Shelf Act 1964 as an area within which the rights of the United Kingdom with respect to the seabed and subsoil and their natural resources may be exercised;
"mariner" means a person who is employed under a contract of service either as a master or member of the crew of any ship or vessel, or in any other capacity on board any ship or vessel, where–
(a) the employment in that capacity is for the purposes of that ship or vessel or its crew or any passengers or cargo or mails carried by the ship or vessel; and

(b) the contract is entered into in the United Kingdom with a view to its performance (in whole or in part) while the ship or vessel is on its voyage;";

(bb) after the definition of "medically approved" insert–

""member of Her Majesty's forces posted overseas" means a person who is a member of the regular forces or the reserve forces (within the meaning of section 374 of the Armed Forces Act 2006), who is absent from the main dwelling because the person has been posted outside of Great Britain to perform the duties of a member of Her Majesty's regular forces or reserve forces;"; and

(cc) after the definition of "patient" insert–

""prescribed area" means any area over which Norway or any member State (other than the United Kingdom) exercises sovereign rights for the purpose of exploring the seabed and subsoil and exploiting their natural resources, being an area outside the territorial seas of Norway or such member State, or any other area which is from time to time specified under section 10(8) of the Petroleum Act 1998;";

(b) in paragraph 8 (non-dependant deductions)–
   (i) in sub-paragraph (1)(a) for "£11.45" substitute "£11.55";
   (ii) in sub-paragraph (1)(b) for "£3.77" substitute "£3.80";
   (iii) in sub-paragraph (2)(a) for "£195.00" substitute "£196.95";
   (iv) in sub-paragraph (2)(b) for "£195.00", "£338.00" and "£7.58" substitute "£196.95", "£341.40" and "£7.65" respectively;
   (v) in sub-paragraph (2)(c) for "£338.00", "£420.00" and "£9.56" substitute "£341.40", "£424.20" and "£9.65" respectively;
(c) in paragraph 19(5)(a) (calculation of net earnings of employed earners)–
   (i) after "basic rate" in the first place it appears insert ", or in the case of a Scottish taxpayer, the Scottish basic rate,";
   (ii) for "personal relief to which the applicant is entitled under section 35, 36 or 37 of the Income Tax Act 2007 as is" substitute "personal reliefs to which the applicant is entitled under Chapters 2, 3 and 3A of Part 3 of the Income Tax Act 2007 as are";
   (iii) after "basic rate" in the second place it appears insert ", or the Scottish basic rate,";
   (iv) for "relief" in the second place it appears substitute "reliefs";
(d) in paragraph 28 (disregard of changes in tax, contributions etc.)–
   (i) after sub-paragraph (a) insert–
      "(aa) in the Scottish basic or other rates of income tax;";
   (ii) in sub-paragraph (b) for "relief" substitute "reliefs under Chapters 2, 3, and 3A of Part 3 of the Income Tax Act 2007";
(e) in paragraph 30 (calculation of deduction of tax and contributions of self-employed earners)–
   (i) in sub-paragraph (1)(b)–
      (aa) after "basic rate" insert ", or in the case of a Scottish taxpayer, the Scottish basic rate,";
      (bb) for "personal relief to which the applicant is entitled under section 35, 36 or 37 of the Income Tax Act 2007 (personal allowances) as is" substitute "personal reliefs to which the applicant is entitled under Chapters 2, 3 and 3A of Part 3 of the Income Tax Act 2007 as are";
   (ii) in sub-paragraph (2) after "basic rate" insert ", or the Scottish basic rate"
(4) In Schedule 2 (applicable amounts)–
(a) in column (2) of the Table in paragraph 1 (personal allowance)–
   (i) in sub-paragraph (1)(a) for "£155.60" substitute "£159.35";
   (ii) in sub-paragraph (1)(b) for "£168.70" substitute "£172.55";

(iii) in sub-paragraph (2)(a) for "£237.55" substitute "£243.25";
(iv) in sub-paragraph (2)(b) for "£252.30" substitute "£258.15";
(v) in sub-paragraph (3)(a) for "£237.55" substitute "£243.25";
(vi) in sub-paragraph (3)(b) for "£81.95" substitute "£83.90";
(vii) in sub-paragraph (4)(a) for "£252.30" substitute "£258.15";
(viii) in sub-paragraph (4)(b) for "£83.60" substitute "£85.60";
(b) in the second column of the Table in Part 4 (amounts of premium specified in Part 3)–
(i) in paragraph (1)(a) and (b)(i) for "£61.85" substitute "£62.45";
(ii) in paragraph (1)(b)(ii) for "£123.70" substitute "£124.90";
(iii) in paragraph (2) for "£24.43" substitute "£24.78";
(iv) in paragraph (3) for "£60.06" substitute "£60.90";
(v) in paragraph (4) for "£34.60" substitute "£34.95".
(5) In column (1) of the Table in paragraph 1 of Schedule 3 (amount of alternative maximum council tax reduction)–
(a) in paragraph (b)(i) for "£193.00" substitute "£194.95";
(b) in paragraph (b)(ii) for "£193.00" and "£250.00" substitute "£194.95" and "£252.50" respectively.

Transitional provision
3.–(1) Subject to paragraph (2), the amendments made by regulation 2(3)(a), shall not apply in respect of a person who is temporarily absent from Great Britain on 1st April 2017 until the day that person returns to Great Britain.
(2) Paragraph (1) does not apply to a person who, on 1st April 2017, is temporarily absent from Great Britain and is–
(a) a member of Her Majesty's forces posted overseas;
(b) absent in the capacity of a continental shelf worker; or
(c) absent in the capacity of a mariner.
(3) In this regulation–
"continental shelf worker" means a person who is employed, whether under a contract of service or not, in a designated area or a prescribed area in connection with any of the activities mentioned in section 11(2) of the Petroleum Act 1998;
"designated area" means any area which may from time to time be designated by Order in Council under the Continental Shelf Act 1964 as an area within which the rights of the United Kingdom with respect to the seabed and subsoil and their natural resources may be exercised;
"mariner" means a person who is employed under a contract of service either as a master or member of the crew of any ship or vessel, or in any other capacity on board any ship or vessel, where–
(a) the employment in that capacity is for the purposes of that ship or vessel or its crew or any passengers or cargo or mails carried by the ship or vessel; and
(b) the contract is entered into in the United Kingdom with a view to its performance (in whole or in part) while the ship or vessel is on its voyage;
"member of Her Majesty's forces posted overseas" means a person who is a member of the regular forces or the reserve forces (within the meaning of section 374 of the Armed Forces Act 2006), who is absent from the dwelling that the person normally occupies as his home because the person has been posted outside of Great Britain to perform the duties of a member of Her Majesty's regular forces or reserve forces; and
"prescribed area" means any area over which Norway or any member State (other than the United Kingdom) exercises sovereign rights for the purpose of exploring the seabed and subsoil and exploiting their natural resources, being an area outside the territorial seas of Norway or such member State, or any other area which is from time to time specified under section 10(8) of the Petroleum Act 1998.

The Council Tax Reduction Schemes (Prescribed Requirements and Default Scheme) (Wales) (Amendment) Regulations 2017

(2017 No.46 (W. 20))

Made   18 January 2017
Coming into force in accordance with regulation 1(2)

The Welsh Ministers make the following Regulations in exercise of the powers conferred upon them by section 13A(4) and (5) of, and paragraphs 2 to 7 of Schedule 1B to, the Local Government Finance Act 1992.

In accordance with section 13A(8) of that Act, a draft of this instrument has been laid before and approved by resolution of the National Assembly for Wales.

Title, commencement and interpretation
1.–(1) The title of these Regulations is the Council Tax Reduction Schemes (Prescribed Requirements and Default Scheme) (Wales) (Amendment) Regulations 2017.
    (2) These Regulations come into force the day after the day on which they are made.
    (3) These Regulations apply in relation to a council tax reduction scheme made for a financial year beginning on or after 1 April 2017.
    (4) In these Regulations "council tax reduction scheme" ("cynllun gostyngiadau'r dreth gyngor") means a scheme made by a billing authority in accordance with the Council Tax Reduction Schemes and Prescribed Requirements (Wales) Regulations 2013, or the scheme that applies in default by virtue of paragraph 6(1)(e) of Schedule 1B to the Local Government Finance Act 1992.

Amendments to the Council Tax Reduction Schemes and Prescribed Requirements (Wales) Regulations 2013
2. The Council Tax Reduction Schemes and Prescribed Requirements (Wales) Regulations 2013 are amended in accordance with regulations 3 to 6.

Amendments to the Council Tax Reduction Schemes and Prescribed Requirements (Wales) Regulations 2013
3. In Schedule 1 (determining eligibility for a reduction: pensioners)–
    (a) in paragraph 3 (non-dependant deductions: pensioners)–
        (i) in sub-paragraph (1)(a) for "£12.25" substitute "£12.70";
        (ii) in sub-paragraph (1)(b) for "£4.05" substitute "£4.20";
        (iii) in sub-paragraph (2)(a) of the Welsh language version for "£195.00" substitute "£200.00";
        (iv) in sub-paragraph (2)(a) of the English language version for "£194.00" substitute "£200.00";
        (v) in sub-paragraph (2)(b) of the Welsh language version for "£195.00", "£338.00" and "£8.10" substitute "£200.00", "£346.00" and "£8.40" respectively;
        (vi) in sub-paragraph (2)(b) of the English language version for "£194.00", "£338.00" and "£8.10" substitute "£200.00", "£346.00" and "£8.40" respectively;
        (vii) in sub-paragraph (2)(c) for "£338.00", "£420.00" and "£10.25" substitute "£346.00", "£430.00" and "£10.60" respectively;
    (b) in paragraph 11 (calculation of weekly income: pensioners)–
        (i) in sub-paragraph (1) for "sub-paragraph (2) or (4)" substitute "sub-paragraph (2), (3A), (4A) or (5)";
        (ii) after sub-paragraph (3) insert–

"(3A) Income calculated pursuant to sub-paragraphs (2) and (3) must be taken into account–

(a) in the case of an application, on the date on which the application was made or treated as made, and the first day of each reduction week thereafter, regardless of whether those earnings were actually received in that reduction week;
(b) in the case of an application or a reduction under a scheme where the applicant commences employment, the first day of the reduction week following the date the applicant commences that employment, and the first day of each reduction week thereafter, regardless of whether those earnings were actually received in that reduction week; or
(c) in the case of an application or a reduction under a scheme where the applicant's average weekly earnings from employment change, the first day of the reduction week following the date the applicant's earnings from employment change so as to require recalculation under this paragraph, and the first day of each reduction week thereafter, regardless of whether those earnings were actually received in that reduction week.";

(iii) after sub-paragraph (4) insert–

"(4A) An applicant's earnings from employment as an employed earner not calculated pursuant to sub-paragraphs (2) and (3) must be taken into account–
(a) in the case of an application, on the date on which the application was made or treated as made, and the first day of each reduction week thereafter, regardless of whether those earnings were actually received in that reduction week;
(b) in the case of an application or a reduction under a scheme where the applicant commences employment, the first day of the reduction week following the date the applicant commences that employment, and the first day of each reduction week thereafter, regardless of whether those earnings were actually received in that reduction week; or
(c) in the case of an application or a reduction under a scheme where the applicant's average weekly earnings from employment change, the first day of the reduction week following the date of the change, and the beginning of each reduction week thereafter, regardless of whether those earnings were actually received in that reduction week.";

(c) in paragraph 13(5)(a) (calculation of net earnings of employed earners: pensioners)–
   (i) for "personal relief to which the applicant is entitled under section 35, 36 or 37" substitute "personal reliefs to which the applicant is entitled under Chapters 2, 3 and 3A of Part 3";
   (ii) omit "(personal allowances)";
   (iii) for "relief" in the second place it occurs substitute "reliefs";
(d) in paragraph 22(b) (disregard of changes in tax, contributions etc) for "relief" substitute "reliefs under Chapters 2, 3 and 3A of Part 3 of the Income Tax Act 2007";
(e) in paragraph 24(1)(b) (calculation of deduction of tax and contributions of self-employed earners) for "personal relief to which the applicant is entitled under section 35, 36 or 37" substitute "personal reliefs to which the applicant is entitled under Chapters 2, 3 and 3A of Part 3".

Amendments to the Council Tax Reduction Schemes and Prescribed Requirements (Wales) Regulations 2013

4. In Schedule 2 (applicable amounts: pensioners)–
(a) in column (2) of the Table in paragraph 1 (personal allowances)–
   (i) in the Welsh language version–
      (aa) in sub-paragraph (1) for "£155.60" and "£168.70" substitute "£159.35" and "£172.55" respectively;
      (bb) in sub-paragraph (2) for "£237.55" and "£252.30" substitute "£243.25" and "£258.15" respectively;

                (cc) in sub-paragraph (3) for "£237.55" and "£81.95" substitute "£243.25" and "£83.90" respectively;
                (dd) in sub-paragraph (4) for "£252.30" and "£83.60" substitute "£258.15" and "£85.60" respectively;
        (ii) in the English language version–
                (aa) in sub-paragraph (1) for "£155.60" and "£170.45" substitute "£159.35" and "£172.55" respectively;
                (bb) in sub-paragraph (2) for "£237.55" and "£255.00" substitute "£243.25" and "£258.15" respectively;
                (cc) in sub-paragraph (3) for "£237.55" and "£81.95" substitute "£243.25" and "£83.90" respectively;
                (dd) in sub-paragraph (4) for "£255.50" and "£84.55" substitute "£258.15" and "£85.60" respectively;
    (b) in paragraph 6 (severe disability premium)–
        (i) in sub-paragraph (2)(a)(iii) after "carer's allowance" insert "under section 70 of the SSCBA or has an award of universal credit which includes the carer element under regulation 29 of the Universal Credit Regulations 2013";
        (ii) in the closing words of sub-paragraph (2)(b)–
                (aa) after "carer's allowance" insert "or has an award of universal credit which includes the carer element";
                (bb) after "such an allowance" insert "or has such an award of universal credit";
        (iii) in sub-paragraph (7)(d)–
                (aa) after "carer's allowance" insert "or having an award of universal credit which includes the carer element";
                (bb) after "be so entitled and in receipt" insert "or have such an award of universal credit";
        (iv) in sub-paragraph (8)(a) after "carer's allowance" insert "or an award of universal credit which includes the carer element";
        (v) in sub-paragraph (8)(b)–
                (aa) after "carer's allowance" insert "or having an award of universal credit which includes the carer element";
                (bb) after "that allowance" insert "or had such an award of universal credit";
    (c) in the Table in Part 4 (amounts of premium specified in Part 3)–
        (i) in the first column–
                (aa) in sub-paragraph (1)(b)(i), after "carer's allowance" insert "or who has an award of universal credit which includes the carer element under regulation 29 of the Universal Credit Regulations 2013,";
                (bb) in sub-paragraph (1)(b)(ii), after "such an allowance" insert "or such an award of universal credit";
        (ii) in the second column–
                (aa) in sub-paragraph (1) for "£61.85" in each place where it occurs substitute "£62.45" and for "£123.70" substitute "£124.90";
                (bb) in sub-paragraph (2) for "£24.43" substitute "£24.78";
                (cc) in sub-paragraph (3) for "£60.06" substitute "£60.90";
                (dd) in sub-paragraph (4) for "£34.60" substitute "£34.95".

Amendments to the Council Tax Reduction Schemes and Prescribed Requirements (Wales) Regulations 2013

5. In Schedule 6 (determining eligibility for a reduction: persons who are not pensioners)–
    (a) in paragraph 5 (non-dependant deductions: persons who are not pensioners)–
        (i) in sub-paragraph (1)(a) for "£12.25" substitute "£12.70";
        (ii) in sub-paragraph (1)(b) for "£4.05" substitute "£4.20";

(iii) in sub-paragraph (2)(a) of the Welsh language version for "£195.00" substitute "£200.00";
(iv) in sub-paragraph (2)(a) of the English language version for "£194.00" substitute "£200.00";
(v) in sub-paragraph (2)(b) of the Welsh language version for "£195.00", "£338.00" and "£8.10" substitute "£200.00", "£346.00" and "£8.40" respectively;
(vi) in sub-paragraph (2)(b) of the English language version for "£194.00", "£338.00" and "£8.10" substitute "£200.00", "£346.00" and "£8.40" respectively;
(vii) in sub-paragraph (2)(c) for "£338.00", "£420.00" and "£10.25" substitute "£346.00", "£430.00" and "£10.60" respectively;
(b) in paragraph 10(2)(a) (average weekly earnings of employed earners: persons who are not pensioners) after "if the applicant has received any earnings" insert "or expects to receive an amount of earnings";
(c) after paragraph 10 insert–

"Date on which income consisting of earnings from employment as an employed earner are taken into account: persons who are not pensioners
10A. An applicant's average weekly earnings from employment estimated pursuant to paragraph 10 (average weekly earnings of employed earners: persons who are not pensioners) and paragraphs 14 and 15 (earnings of employed earners: persons who are not pensioners) of this Schedule must be taken into account–
(a) in the case of an application, on the date on which the application was made or treated as made, and the first day of each reduction week thereafter, regardless of whether those earnings were actually received in that reduction week;
(b) in the case of an application or a reduction under a scheme where the applicant commences employment, the first day of the reduction week following the date the applicant commences that employment, and the first day of each reduction week thereafter, regardless of whether those earnings were actually received in that reduction week; or
(c) in the case of an application or reduction under a scheme where the applicant's average weekly earnings from employment change, the first day of the reduction week following the date of the change, and the beginning of each reduction week thereafter, regardless of whether those earnings were actually received in that reduction week.";
(d) in paragraph 15(6)(a) (calculation of net earnings of employed earners: persons who are not pensioners)–
(i) for "personal relief to which the applicant is entitled under sections 35 to 37" substitute "personal reliefs to which the applicant is entitled under Chapters 2, 3 and 3A of Part 3";
(ii) omit "(personal allowances)";
(iii) for "relief" in the second place it occurs substitute "reliefs";
(e) in paragraph 19(10)(a) (notional income: persons who are not pensioners)–
(i) for "personal relief to which the applicant is entitled under sections 35 to 37" substitute "personal reliefs to which the applicant is entitled under Chapters 2, 3 and 3A of Part 3";
(ii) omit "(personal allowances)";
(iii) for "relief" in the second place it occurs substitute "reliefs";
(f) in paragraph 23(b) (disregard of changes in tax, contributions etc) for "relief" substitute "reliefs under Chapters 2, 3 and 3A of Part 3 of the Income Tax Act 2007";
(g) in paragraph 25(1)(b) (calculation of deduction of tax and contributions of self-employed earners)–
(i) for "personal relief to which the applicant is entitled under section 35 to 37" substitute "personal reliefs to which the applicant is entitled under Chapters 2, 3 and 3A of Part 3";
(ii) omit "(personal allowances)".

Amendments to the Council Tax Reduction Schemes and Prescribed Requirements (Wales) Regulations 2013

6. In Schedule 7 (applicable amounts: persons who are not pensioners)–
   (a) in column (2) of the Table in paragraph 1 (personal allowances)–
      (i) in sub-paragraph (1) for "£73.10" in each place in which it occurs substitute "£73.85" and for "£57.90" substitute "£58.50";
      (ii) in sub-paragraph (2) for "£73.10" substitute "£73.85";
      (iii) in sub-paragraph (3) for "£114.85" substitute "£116.00";
   (b) in paragraph 11 (severe disability premium)–
      (i) in sub-paragraph (2)(a)(iii) after "SSCBA" insert "or has an award of universal credit which includes the carer element under regulation 29 of the Universal Credit Regulations 2013";
      (ii) in the closing words of sub-paragraph (2)(b)–
         (aa) after "carer's allowance" insert "or has an award of universal credit which includes the carer element";
         (bb) after "such an allowance" insert "or has such an award of universal credit";
      (iii) in sub-paragraph (5)(b)–
         (aa) after "carer's allowance" insert "or having an award of universal credit which includes the carer element";
         (bb) after "be so entitled and in receipt" insert "or have such an award of universal credit";
      (iv) in sub-paragraph (6) after "carer's allowance" insert "or an award of universal credit which includes the carer element";
      (v) in sub-paragraph (7)–
         (aa) after "carer's allowance" insert "or having an award of universal credit which includes the carer element";
         (bb) after "that allowance" insert "or had such an award of universal credit";
   (c) in the Table in Part 4 (amounts of premiums specified in Part 3)–
      (i) in the first column–
         (aa) in sub-paragraph (2)(b)(i), after "carer's allowance" insert "or who has an award of universal credit which includes the carer element under regulation 29 of the Universal Credit Regulations 2013,";
         (bb) in sub-paragraph (2)(b)(ii), after "such an allowance" insert "or such an award of universal credit";
      (ii) in the second column–
         (aa) in sub-paragraph (1) for "£32.25" and "£45.95" substitute "£32.55" and "£46.40" respectively;
         (bb) in sub-paragraph (2) for "£61.85" in each place in which it occurs substitute "£62.45" and for "£123.70" substitute "£124.90";
         (cc) in sub-paragraph (3) for "£60.06" substitute "£60.90";
         (dd) in sub-paragraph (4) for "£34.60" substitute "£34.95";
         (ee) in sub-paragraph (5) for "£24.43", "£15.75" and "£22.60" substitute "£24.78", "£15.90" and "£22.85" respectively;
   (d) in paragraph 23 (amount of work-related activity component), for "£29.05" substitute "£29.35";
   (e) in paragraph 24 (amount of support component), for "£36.20" substitute "£36.55".

Amendments to the Council Tax Reduction Schemes (Default Scheme) (Wales) Regulations 2013

7. The scheme set out in the Schedule to the Council Tax Reduction Schemes (Default Scheme) (Wales) Regulations 2013 is amended in accordance with regulations 8 to 18.

(SI 2017 No.46, reg 9)

Amendments to the Council Tax Reduction Schemes (Default Scheme) (Wales) Regulations 2013

8. In paragraph 28 (non-dependant deductions: pensioners and persons who are not pensioners)–
- (a) in sub-paragraph (1)(a) for "£12.25" substitute "£12.70";
- (b) in sub-paragraph (1)(b) for "£4.05" substitute "£4.20";
- (c) in sub-paragraph (2)(a) of the Welsh language version for "£195.00" substitute "£200.00";
- (d) in sub-paragraph (2)(a) of the English language version for "£194.00" substitute "£200.00";
- (e) in sub-paragraph (2)(b) of the Welsh language version for "£195.00", "£338.00" and "£8.10" substitute "£200.00", "£346.00" and "£8.40" respectively;
- (f) in sub-paragraph (2)(b) of the English language version for "£194.00", "£338.00" and "£8.10" substitute "£200.00", "£346.00" and "£8.40" respectively;
- (g) in sub-paragraph (2)(c) for "£338.00", "£420.00" and "£10.25" substitute "£346.00", "£430.00" and "£10.60" respectively.

Amendments to the Council Tax Reduction Schemes (Default Scheme) (Wales) Regulations 2013

9. In paragraph 37 (calculation of weekly income: pensioners)–
- (a) in sub-paragraph (1) for "sub-paragraph (2) or (4)" substitute "sub-paragraph (2), (3A), (4A) or (5)";
- (b) after sub-paragraph (3) insert–

"(3A) Income calculated pursuant to sub-paragraphs (2) and (3) must be taken into account–
- (a) in the case of an application, on the date on which the application was made or treated as made, and the first day of each reduction week thereafter, regardless of whether those earnings were actually received in that reduction week;
- (b) in the case of an application or a reduction under a scheme where the applicant commences employment, the first day of the reduction week following the date the applicant commences that employment, and the first day of each reduction week thereafter, regardless of whether those earnings were actually received in that reduction week; or
- (c) in the case of an application or a reduction under a scheme where the applicant's average weekly earnings from employment change, the first day of the reduction week following the date the applicant's earnings from employment change so as to require recalculation under this paragraph, and the first day of each reduction week thereafter, regardless of whether those earnings were actually received in that reduction week.";

- (c) after sub-paragraph (4) insert–

"(4A) An applicant's earnings from employment as an employed earner not calculated pursuant to sub-paragraphs (2) and (3) must be taken into account–
- (a) in the case of an application, on the date on which the application was made or treated as made, and the first day of each reduction week thereafter, regardless of whether those earnings were actually received in that reduction week;
- (b) in the case of an application or a reduction under a scheme where the applicant commences employment, the first day of the reduction week following the date the applicant commences that employment, and the first day of each reduction week thereafter, regardless of whether those earnings were actually received in that reduction week; or
- (c) in the case of an application or a reduction under a scheme where the applicant's average weekly earnings from employment change, the first day of the reduction week following the date of the change, and the beginning of each reduction week thereafter, regardless of whether those earnings were actually received in that reduction week."

Amendments to the Council Tax Reduction Schemes (Default Scheme) (Wales) Regulations 2013

10. In paragraph 39(5)(a) (calculation of net earnings of employed earners: pensioners)–
(a) for "personal relief to which the applicant is entitled under sections 35 to 37" substitute "personal reliefs to which the applicant is entitled under Chapters 2, 3 and 3A of Part 3";
(b) omit "(personal allowances)";
(c) for "relief" in the second place it occurs substitute "reliefs".

Amendments to the Council Tax Reduction Schemes (Default Scheme) (Wales) Regulations 2013

11. In paragraph 44(2)(a) (average weekly earnings of employed earners: persons who are not pensioners) after "if the applicant has received any earnings" insert "or expects to receive an amount of earnings".

Amendments to the Council Tax Reduction Schemes (Default Scheme) (Wales) Regulations 2013

12. After paragraph 44 insert–

"Date on which income consisting of earnings from employment as an employed earner are taken into account: persons who are not pensioners

44A. An applicant's average weekly earnings from employment estimated pursuant to paragraph 44 (average weekly earnings of employed earners: persons who are not pensioners) and paragraphs 48 and 49 (earnings of employed earners: persons who are not pensioners) must be taken into account–
(a) in the case of an application, on the date on which the application was made or treated as made, and the first day of each reduction week thereafter, regardless of whether those earnings were actually received in that reduction week;
(b) in the case of an application or a reduction under a scheme where the applicant commences employment, the first day of the reduction week following the date the applicant commences that employment, and the first day of each reduction week thereafter, regardless of whether those earnings were actually received in that reduction week; or
(c) in the case of an application or reduction under a scheme where the applicant's average weekly earnings from employment change, the first day of the reduction week following the date of the change, and the beginning of each reduction week thereafter, regardless of whether those earnings were actually received in that reduction week."

Amendments to the Council Tax Reduction Schemes (Default Scheme) (Wales) Regulations 2013

13. In paragraph 49(6)(a) (calculation of net earnings of employed earners: persons who are not pensioners)–
(a) for "personal relief to which the applicant is entitled under sections 35 to 37" substitute "personal reliefs to which the applicant is entitled under Chapters 2, 3 and 3A of Part 3";
(b) omit "(personal allowances)";
(c) for "relief" in the second place it occurs substitute "reliefs".

Amendments to the Council Tax Reduction Schemes (Default Scheme) (Wales) Regulations 2013

14. In paragraph 53(10)(a) (notional income: persons who are not pensioners)–
(a) for "personal relief to which the applicant is entitled under sections 35 to 37" substitute "personal reliefs to which the applicant is entitled under Chapters 2, 3 and 3A";
(b) omit "(personal allowances)";

(SI 2017 No.46, reg 17)

(c) for "relief" in the second place it occurs substitute "reliefs".

Amendments to the Council Tax Reduction Schemes (Default Scheme) (Wales) Regulations 2013
15. In paragraph 57(b) (disregard of changes in tax, contributions etc) for "relief" substitute "reliefs under Chapters 2, 3 and 3A of Part 3 of the Income Tax Act 2007".

Amendments to the Council Tax Reduction Schemes (Default Scheme) (Wales) Regulations 2013
16. In paragraph 59(1)(b) (calculation of deduction of tax and contributions of self-employed earners)–
(a) for "personal relief to which the applicant is entitled under sections 35 to 37" substitute "personal reliefs to which the applicant is entitled under Chapters 2, 3 and 3A of Part 3";
(b) omit "(personal allowances)".

Amendments to the Council Tax Reduction Schemes (Default Scheme) (Wales) Regulations 2013
17. In Schedule 2 (applicable amounts: pensioners)–
(a) in column (2) of the Table in paragraph 1 (personal allowances)–
  (i) in the Welsh language version–
   (aa) in sub-paragraph (1) for "£155.60" and "£168.70" substitute "£159.35" and "£172.55" respectively;
   (bb) in sub-paragraph (2) for "£237.55" and "£252.30" substitute "£243.25" and "£258.15" respectively;
   (cc) in sub-paragraph (3) for "£237.55" and "£81.95" substitute "£243.25" and "£83.90" respectively;
   (dd) in sub-paragraph (4) for "£252.30" and "£83.60" substitute "£258.15" and "£85.60" respectively;
  (ii) in the English language version–
   (aa) in sub-paragraph (1) for "£155.60" and "£170.45" substitute "£159.35" and "£172.55" respectively;
   (bb) in sub-paragraph (2) for "£237.55" and "£255.00" substitute "£243.25" and "£258.15" respectively;
   (cc) in sub-paragraph (3) for "£237.55" and "£81.95" substitute "£243.25" and "£83.90" respectively;
   (dd) in sub-paragraph (4) for "£255.50" and "£84.55" substitute "£258.15" and "£85.60" respectively;
(b) in paragraph 6 (severe disability premium)–
  (i) in sub-paragraph (2)(a)(iii) after "carer's allowance" insert "under section 70 of the SSCBA or has an award of universal credit which includes the carer element under regulation 29 of the Universal Credit Regulations 2013";
  (ii) in the closing words of sub-paragraph (2)(b)–
   (aa) after "carer's allowance" insert "or has an award of universal credit which includes the carer element";
   (bb) after "such an allowance" insert "or has such an award of universal credit";
  (iii) in sub-paragraph (7)(d)–
   (aa) after "carer's allowance" insert "or having an award of universal credit which includes the carer element";
   (bb) after "be so entitled and in receipt" insert "or have such an award of universal credit";
  (iv) in sub-paragraph (8)(a) after "carer's allowance" insert "or an award of universal credit which includes the carer element";
  (v) in sub-paragraph (8)(b)–

           (aa) after "carer's allowance" insert "or having an award of universal credit which includes the carer element";
           (bb) after "that allowance" insert "or had such an award of universal credit";
    (c) in the Table in Part 4 (amounts of premiums specified in Part 3)–
       (i) in the first column–
           (aa) in sub-paragraph (1)(b)(i), after "carer's allowance" insert "or who has an award of universal credit which includes the carer element under regulation 29 of the Universal Credit Regulations 2013,";
           (bb) in sub-paragraph (1)(b)(ii), after "such an allowance" insert "or such an award of universal credit";
       (ii) in the second column–
           (aa) in sub-paragraph (1) for "£61.85" in each place in which it occurs substitute "£62.45" and for "£123.70" substitute "£124.90";
           (bb) in sub-paragraph (2) for "£24.43" substitute "£24.78";
           (cc) in sub-paragraph (3) for "£60.06" substitute "£60.90";
           (dd) in sub-paragraph (4) for "£34.60" substitute "£34.95".

Amendments to the Council Tax Reduction Schemes (Default Scheme) (Wales) Regulations 2013

18. In Schedule 3 (applicable amounts: persons who are not pensioners)–
 (a) in column (2) of the Table in paragraph 1 (personal allowances)–
       (i) in sub-paragraph (1) for "£73.10" in each place in which it occurs substitute "£73.85" and for "£57.90" substitute "£58.50";
       (ii) in sub-paragraph (2) for "£73.10" substitute "£73.85";
       (iii) in sub-paragraph (3) for "£114.85" substitute "£116.00";
 (b) in paragraph 11 (severe disability premium)–
       (i) in sub-paragraph (2)(a)(iii) after "SSCBA" insert "or has an award of universal credit which includes the carer element under regulation 29 of the Universal Credit Regulations 2013";
       (ii) in the closing words of sub-paragraph (2)(b)–
           (aa) after "carer's allowance" insert "or has an award of universal credit which includes the carer element";
           (bb) after "such an allowance" insert "or has such an award of universal credit";
       (iii) in sub-paragraph (5)(b)–
           (aa) after "carer's allowance" insert "or having an award of universal credit which includes the carer element";
           (bb) after "be so entitled and in receipt" insert "or have such an award of universal credit";
       (iv) in sub-paragraph (6) after "carer's allowance" insert "or an award of universal credit which includes the carer element";
       (v) in sub-paragraph (7)–
           (aa) after "carer's allowance" insert "or having an award of universal credit which includes the carer element";
           (bb) after "that allowance" insert "or had such an award of universal credit";
 (c) in the Table in Part 4 (amounts of premiums specified in Part 3)–
       (i) in the first column–
           (aa) in sub-paragraph (2)(b)(i), after "carer's allowance" insert "or who has an award of universal credit which includes the carer element under regulation 29 of the Universal Credit Regulations 2013,";
           (bb) in sub-paragraph (2)(b)(ii), after "such an allowance" insert "or such an award of universal credit";
       (ii) in the second column–
           (aa) in sub-paragraph (1) for "£32.25" and "£45.95" substitute "£32.55" and "£46.40" respectively;

        (bb) in sub-paragraph (2) for "£61.85" in each place in which it occurs substitute "£62.45" and for "£123.70" substitute "£124.90";
        (cc) in sub-paragraph (3) for "£60.06" substitute "£60.90";
        (dd) in sub-paragraph (4) for "£34.60" substitute "£34.95";
        (ee) in sub-paragraph (5) for "£24.43", "£15.75" and "£22.60" substitute "£24.78", "£15.90" and "£22.85" respectively;
(d) in paragraph 23 (amount of work-related activity component), for "£29.05" substitute "£29.35";
(e) in paragraph 24 (amount of support component), for "£36.20" substitute "£36.55".

The Council Tax Reduction (Scotland) Amendment Regulations 2017
(2017 No.41)

Made   21st February 2017
Laid before the Scottish Parliament   23rd February 2017
Coming into force   1st April 2017

The Scottish Ministers make the following Regulations in exercise of the powers conferred by sections 80 and 113(1) and (2) and paragraph 1 of schedule 2 of the Local Government Finance Act 1992 and all other powers enabling them to do so.

Citation and commencement
1. These Regulations may be cited as the Council Tax Reduction (Scotland) Amendment Regulations 2017 and come into force on 1st April 2017.

General
2. The Council Tax Reduction (Scotland) Regulations 2012 are amended as follows.

Amendment of regulation 2
3. In regulation 2 (interpretation), in paragraph (1) after the definition of "independent hospital" insert–

""infected blood payment scheme" means a scheme established by, or under arrangements made with, the Scottish Ministers, the Secretary of State, the Welsh Ministers or the Department of Health in Northern Ireland for making ex gratia payments to or in respect of persons who have acquired HIV or hepatitis C as a result of treatment with blood or blood products within the national health service;".

Amendment of regulation 23
4. In regulation 23 (applicable amount: persons who have an award of universal credit)–
 (a) in paragraph (1), for "adjustment" substitute "adjustments"; and
 (b) for paragraph (2A), substitute–

"(2A) The adjustments referred to in paragraph (1) are–
 (a) to multiply the maximum amount by 12 and divide the product by 52; and
 (b) to add to the weekly applicable amount the sum of £16.73 in respect of each child or young person who is a member of the applicant's family.".

Amendment of regulation 41
5. In regulation 41 (notional income), in paragraph (4)(a) after "Foundation," insert "another infected blood payment scheme,".

Amendment of regulation 45
6. In regulation 45 (income treated as capital), in paragraph (6) after "Foundation," insert "another infected blood payment scheme,".

Amendment of regulation 48
7. In regulation 48 (notional capital), in paragraph (4)(a) after "Foundation," insert "another infected blood payment scheme,".

Amendment of regulation 67
8. In regulation 67 (non-dependant deductions)–
 (a) in paragraph (1)–
  (i) in sub-paragraph (a), for "£11.80" substitute "£11.90"; and

(SI 2017 No.41, reg 14)

       (ii)   in sub-paragraph (b), for "£3.90" substitute "£3.95";
(b)   in paragraph (2)–
       (i)   in sub-paragraph (a), for "£195.00" substitute "£200.00"; and
       (ii)   for sub-paragraphs (b) and (c), substitute–

"(b)   not less than £200.00 but less than £346.00, the deduction to be made is £7.85 x 1/7; or
(c)   not less than £346.00 but less than £430.00, the deduction to be made is £9.95 x 1/7."; and

(c)   in paragraph (9)(b), after "Foundation," insert "another infected blood payment scheme,".

Amendment of regulation 86
9. In regulation 86 (evidence and information), in paragraph (3)(a)(ii) after "Foundation" insert ", another infected blood payment scheme".

Amendment of schedule 1
10. In schedule 1 (applicable amount)–
(a)   in paragraph 17 (amounts of disability premiums)–
       (i)   for "£32.25", substitute "£32.55";
       (ii)   for "£45.95", substitute "£46.40";
       (iii)   for "£61.85" in both places where it occurs, substitute "£62.45";
       (iv)   for "£123.70", substitute "£124.90";
       (v)   for "£60.06", substitute "£60.90";
       (vi)   for "£34.60", substitute "£34.95";
       (vii)   for "£24.43", substitute "£24.78";
       (viii)   for "£15.75", substitute "£15.90"; and
       (ix)   for "£22.60", substitute "£22.85"; and
(b)   in paragraph 24 (amount of the support component), for "£36.20" substitute "£36.55".

Amendment of schedule 2
11. In schedule 2 (amount of alternative maximum council tax reduction)–
(a)   in paragraph 1–
       (i)   for "£191.00" in both places where it occurs, substitute "£196.00"; and
       (ii)   for "£249.00", substitute "£255.00"; and
(b)   in paragraph 2(b), after "Foundation," insert "another infected blood payment scheme,".

Amendment of schedule 4
12. In schedule 4 (sums to be disregarded in the calculation of income other than earnings), in paragraph 41–
(a)   in sub-paragraph (1), after "Foundation," insert "another infected blood payment scheme,"; and
(b)   in sub-paragraph (7), after "Foundation," insert "any other infected blood payment scheme,".

Amendment of schedule 5
13. In schedule 5 (capital to be disregarded), in paragraph 38 after "Foundation," insert "another infected blood payment scheme,".

General
14. The Council Tax Reduction (State Pension Credit) (Scotland) Regulations 2012 are amended as follows.

Amendment of regulation 2
15. In regulation 2 (interpretation), in paragraph (1) after the definition of "independent hospital" insert–

""infected blood payment scheme" means a scheme established by, or under arrangements made with, the Scottish Ministers, the Secretary of State, the Welsh Ministers or the Department of Health in Northern Ireland for making ex gratia payments to or in respect of persons who have acquired HIV or hepatitis C as a result of treatment with blood or blood products within the national health service;".

Amendment of regulation 48
16. In regulation 48 (non-dependant deductions)–
(a) in paragraph (1)–
  (i) in sub-paragraph (a), for "£11.80" substitute "£11.90"; and
  (ii) in sub-paragraph (b), for "£3.90" substitute "£3.95";
(b) in paragraph (2)–
  (i) in sub-paragraph (a), for "£195.00" substitute "£200.00"; and
  (ii) for sub-paragraphs (b) and (c), substitute–

"(b) not less than £200.00 but less than £346.00, the deduction to be made is £7.85 x 1/7; and
(c) not less than £346.00 but less than £430.00, the deduction to be made is £9.95 x 1/7."; and

(c) in paragraph (9)(b), after "Foundation," insert "another infected blood payment scheme,".

Amendment of regulation 66
17. In regulation 66 (evidence and information), in paragraph (3)(a) after "Foundation" insert ", another infected blood payment scheme".

Amendment of schedule 1
18. In schedule 1 (applicable amount)–
(a) in paragraph 2 (personal allowances)–
  (i) for "£155.60", substitute "£159.35";
  (ii) for "£168.70", substitute "£172.55";
  (iii) for "£237.55" in both places where it occurs, substitute "£243.25";
  (iv) for "£252.30" in both places where it occurs, substitute "£258.15";
  (v) for "£81.95", substitute "£83.90"; and
  (vi) for "£83.60", substitute "£85.60"; and
(b) in paragraph 13 (amount of disability premium)–
  (i) for "£61.85" in both places where it occurs, substitute "£62.45";
  (ii) for "£123.70", substitute "£124.90";
  (iii) for "£24.43", substitute "£24.78";
  (iv) for "£60.06", substitute "£60.90"; and
  (v) for "£34.60", substitute "£34.95".

Amendment of schedule 4
19. In schedule 4 (capital disregards), in paragraph 16–
(a) in sub-paragraph (1)(a), after "Foundation" insert ", another infected blood payment scheme";
(b) in sub-paragraph (7), after "Foundation" insert ", another infected blood payment scheme"; and
(c) in sub-paragraph (8), after "Foundation" insert ", any other infected blood payment scheme".

Amendment of schedule 5
20. In schedule 5 (amount of alternative maximum council tax reduction)–
(a) in paragraph 1–
  (i) for "£191.00" in both places where it occurs, substitute "£196.00"; and
  (ii) for "£249.00", substitute "£255.00"; and
(b) in paragraph 2(b), after "Foundation," insert "another infected blood payment scheme,".

The Valuation Tribunal for England (Council Tax and Rating Appeals) (Procedure) (Amendment) Regulations 2017

(2017 No.156)

Made   16th March 2017
Laid before Parliament   17th March 2017
Coming into force   1st April 2017

The Secretary of State, in exercise of the powers conferred by sections 55(2) to (6) and 143(1) and (2) of, and paragraphs A19, 8 and 16 of Schedule 11 to the Local Government Finance Act 1988, makes the following Regulations.

Citation and commencement
1.–(1) These Regulations may be cited as the Valuation Tribunal for England (Council Tax and Rating Appeals) (Procedure) (Amendment) Regulations 2017.
(2) These Regulations come into force on 1st April 2017.

Application
2. The amendments made by these Regulations apply only in relation to–
(a) a local non-domestic rating list compiled on or after 1st April 2017; and
(b) a central non-domestic rating list compiled on or after 1st April 2017.

Interpretation
3. In these Regulations "the 2009 Procedure Regulations" means the Valuation Tribunal for England (Council Tax and Rating Appeals) (Procedure) Regulations 2009.

Amendment of regulation 2
4. In regulation 2 (interpretation: general) of the 2009 Procedure Regulations–
(a) in paragraph (1)—
 (i) in the definition of "appeal", for paragraph (c) substitute–

"(c) regulation 13A of the NDR Regulations;"; and

 (ii) after the definition of "local list" insert–

""NDR appeal" means an appeal under regulation 13A of the NDR Regulations;";

(b) in paragraph (3)(d)(i)–
 (i) for "regulation 8, 13" substitute "regulation 13A"; and
 (ii) for "VO" substitute "VTE"; and
(c) after paragraph (3) insert–

"(4) A reference in these Regulations to a matter included in the notice of appeal or any document accompanying the notice of appeal does not include any particulars of the grounds of the proposal with which the VO agreed.
(5) In paragraph (4), "particulars of the grounds of the proposal" has the meaning given in the NDR Regulations.".

Amendment of regulation 6
6. In regulation 6 (appeal management powers) of the 2009 Procedure Regulations–
(a) in paragraph (3)(c), before "permit" insert "subject to paragraph (4),";
(b) in paragraph (3)(d), before "permit" insert "subject to regulations 17, 17A and 18A,";
(c) after paragraph (3) insert–

"(4) The VTE may permit or require a party to a NDR appeal to amend a document under paragraph (3)(c) only if the amendment is in order to correct an inaccuracy in the document.".

Amendment of regulation 17
8. In regulation 17 (evidence and submissions) of the 2009 Procedure Regulations–
(a) in paragraph (1), for "The VTE" substitute "Subject to paragraph (1A), the VTE";
(b) after paragraph (1) insert–

"(1A) The VTE may only direct a party to a NDR appeal to provide evidence or submissions that relate to a matter included in–
(a) the notice of appeal or any document accompanying the notice of appeal; or
(b) new or further evidence admitted under regulation 17A.";

(c) in paragraph (2), for "The VTE" substitute "Subject to regulation 17A, the VTE";
(d) in paragraph (4), at the end insert–

"(c) for a NDR appeal, the information relates to a matter included in–
  (i) the notice of appeal or any document accompanying the notice of appeal; or
  (ii) new or further evidence admitted under regulation 17A."; and

(e) after paragraph (6) insert–

"(6A) On a NDR appeal, the VTE may only admit as evidence documents produced or submitted under paragraph (6)(b) that relate to a matter included in–
(a) the notice of appeal or any document accompanying the notice of appeal; or
(b) new or further evidence admitted under regulation 17A.".

Amendment of regulation 18
10. In regulation 18 (summoning of witnesses, and orders to answer questions or produce documents) of the 2009 Procedure Regulations, before paragraph (1) insert–

"(A1) In relation to a NDR appeal, this regulation applies subject to regulation 18A.".

Amendment of regulation 36
14. In regulation 36 (notice of decisions) of the 2009 Procedure Regulations, after paragraph (2) insert–

"(3) For a NDR appeal–
(a) a decision notice provided under paragraph (2)(a) must be accompanied by a written statement of the VTE panel's reasons for the decision;
(b) the statement of reasons for the decision must specify which, if any, grounds of the appeal were made out; and
(c) the VTE must send a copy of the decision notice and the statement of reasons for the decision to–
  (i) if the appellant is not the ratepayer, the ratepayer; and
  (ii) any IP mentioned in regulation 12(2)(e) of the NDR Regulations who was served a notice of the VO's decision under regulation 13(2) of those Regulations.
(4) In paragraph (3)(b), "grounds of the appeal" has the meaning given in regulation 2 of the NDR Regulations.".

The Social Security (Income-Related Benefits) Amendment Regulations 2017

(2017 No.174)

Made 20th February 2017
Laid before Parliament 23rd February 2017
Coming into force 20th March 2017

The Secretary of State for Work and Pensions, in exercise of the powers conferred by sections 136 (5)(b), 137(1) and 175(1) and (3) of the Social Security Contributions and Benefits Act 1992, sections 12(4)(b), 35(1) and 36(2) of the Jobseekers Act 1995, sections 15(1)(j) and (6)(b), 17(1) and 19(1) of the State Pension Credit Act 2002 and sections 17(3)(b), 24(1) and 25(2) and (3) of the Welfare Reform Act 2007 makes the following Regulations.

The Social Security Advisory Committee has agreed that proposals in respect of these Regulations should not be referred to it.

In accordance with section 176(1) of the Social Security Administration Act 1992, the Secretary of State has consulted with organisations appearing to him to be representative of the authorities concerned.

Citation and commencement
1. These Regulations may be cited as the Social Security (Income-Related Benefits) Amendment Regulations 2017 and come into force on 20th March 2017.

The Housing Benefit Regulations 2006
5. For paragraph 15(g) of Schedule 5 (sums to be disregarded in the calculation of income other than earnings) to the Housing Benefit Regulations 2006, substitute–

"(g) a pension paid by a government to victims of National Socialist persecution.".

The Housing Benefit (Persons who have attained the qualifying age for state pension credit) Regulations 2006
6.–(1) The Housing Benefit (Persons who have attained the qualifying age for state pension credit) Regulations 2006 are amended as follows.
(2) For regulation 29(1)(m) (meaning of "income"), substitute–

"(m) a pension paid by a government to victims of National Socialist persecution;".

(3) For paragraph 1(g) of Schedule 5 (amounts to be disregarded in the calculation of income other than earnings), substitute–

"(g) a pension paid by a government to victims of National Socialist persecution.".

The Employment and Support Allowance and Universal Credit (Miscellaneous Amendments and Transitional and Savings Provisions) Regulations 2017

(2017 No.204)

Made	23rd February 2017
Laid before Parliament	27th February 2017
Coming into force	3rd April 2017

The Secretary of State for Work and Pensions makes the following Regulations in exercise of the powers conferred by sections 12(1), 17(4), 18(3), 19(2)(d), 25(a) and 42(3)(a) of the Welfare Reform Act 2012 and sections 15(4) and (5) and 34(1) of the Welfare Reform and Work Act 2016.

In accordance with section 173(5)(b) of the Social Security Administration Act 1992, this instrument contains only regulations made by virtue of, or consequential upon, sections 15, 16, 17 and 34 of the Welfare Reform and Work Act 2016 and is made before the end of the period of 6 months beginning with the coming into force of those sections.

In accordance with section 176(1) of the Social Security Administration Act 1992 the Secretary of State has consulted with organisations appearing to him to be representative of the authorities concerned.

Citation and commencement

1. These Regulations may be cited as the Employment and Support Allowance and Universal Credit (Miscellaneous Amendments and Transitional and Savings Provisions) Regulations 2017 and come into force on 3rd April 2017.

Consequential, transitional and savings provisions

7.–(1) Schedule 1 contains amendments to secondary legislation as a consequence of the amendments made by these Regulations.

(2) Schedule 2 contains transitional and savings provisions.

SCHEDULE 1

Consequential amendments to secondary legislation

Regulation 7(1)

PART 1

Employment and Support Allowance: amendments to secondary legislation consequential on removal of work-related activity component

Amendment to the Housing Benefit and Council Tax Benefit (Decisions and Appeals) Regulations 2001

4. In regulation 7 (decisions superseding earlier decisions) of the Housing Benefit and Council Tax Benefit (Decisions and Appeals) Regulations 2001, in paragraph (2)(o)(iv)(bb) omit "or the work-related activity component".

Amendments to the Housing Benefit Regulations 2006

6.–(1) The Housing Benefit Regulations 2006 are amended as follows.

(2) In regulation 2 (interpretation), in paragraph (1) in the appropriate place insert–

""member of the work-related activity group" means a claimant who has or is treated as having limited capability for work under either–
- (a) Part 5 of the Employment and Support Allowance Regulations 2008 other than by virtue of regulation 30 of those Regulations; or
- (b) Part 4 of the Employment and Support Allowance Regulations 2013 other than by virtue of regulation 26 of those Regulations;".

(3) In regulation 22 (applicable amounts) for paragraph (e) substitute–

"(e) the amount of the support component which may be applicable to him in accordance with Part 5 of Schedule 3 (the component);".

(4) In regulation 23 (polygamous marriages) for paragraph (f) substitute–

"(f) the amount of the support component which may be applicable to him in accordance with Part 5 of Schedule 3 (the component);".

(5) In regulation 28 (treatment of child care charges), in paragraph (11)–
(a) in sub-paragraph (a)–
    (i) omit "the work-related activity component";
    (ii) after "support component or" insert "the other member is a member of the work-related activity group";
(b) in sub-paragraph (ba)–
    (i) omit "the work-related activity component";
    (ii) after "support component or" insert "the other member would be a member of the work-related activity group".

(6) In regulation 74 (non-dependant deductions) in paragraph (8)(a)–
(a) omit "and the work-related activity component";
(b) after "(the support component)" insert "or where the non-dependant is not a member of the work-related activity group".

(7) In Schedule 3 (applicable amounts)–
(a) in Part 5 (the components)–
    (i) in the heading, for "components" substitute "component";
    (ii) n paragraph 21, in sub-paragraph (1)–
        (aa) for "one, but not both, of the components in paragraph 23 or" substitute "the component in paragraph";
        (bb) for paragraph (b) substitute–

"(b) the Secretary of State has determined that the claimant or the claimant's partner has or is treated as having limited capability for work-related activity; and";

        (cc) in paragraph (c)(ii) omit "or the work-related activity component";
    (iii) in paragraph 22 in sub-paragraphs (1) and (2) omit "23 or";
    (iv) omit paragraph 23;
(b) in Part 6 (amount of components)–
    (i) in the heading, for "components" substitute "component";
    (ii) omit paragraph 25.

(8) In Schedule 4 (sums to be disregarded in the calculation of earnings)–
(a) in paragraph 3(2)–
    (i) omit ", work-related activity component";
    (ii) after "Schedule 3 (applicable amounts)" insert "or where the claimant or the claimant's partner is a member of the work-related activity group";
(b) in paragraph 17, in sub-paragraph (2)(b)(iv)–
    (i) in paragraph (aa)–
        (aa) omit ", the work-related activity component under paragraph 23 or";
        (bb) after "of Schedule 3" insert "or the claimant or the claimant's partner is a member of the work-related activity group";
    (ii) in paragraph (bb)–
        (aa) omit ", the work-related activity component";
        (bb) after "sub-head (aa) above," insert "or at least one of the couple is a member of the work-related activity group".

Amendments to the Housing Benefit (Persons who have attained the qualifying age for state pension credit) Regulations 2006

7.–(1) The Housing Benefit (Persons who have attained the qualifying age for state pension credit) Regulations 2006 are amended as follows.

(2) In regulation 2 (interpretation), in paragraph (1) in the appropriate place insert–

""member of the work-related activity group" means a claimant who has or is treated as having limited capability for work under either–
(a) Part 5 of the Employment and Support Allowance Regulations 2008 other than by virtue of regulation 30 of those Regulations; or
(b) Part 4 of the Employment and Support Allowance Regulations 2013 other than by virtue of regulation 26 of those Regulations;".

(3) In regulation 31 (treatment of child care charges), in paragraph (11)(ba)–
(a) omit "or the work-related activity component";
(b) after "limited capability for work" insert "or the other member of the couple would be a member of the work-related activity group".

(4) In regulation 55 (non-dependant deductions), in paragraph (8)–
(a) omit "and the work-related activity component";
(b) after "(the support component)" insert "or where the non-dependant is not a member of the work-related activity group".
(5) In Schedule 4 (sums disregarded from claimant's earnings), in paragraph 5(1)(d)(ii) omit "or the work-related activity component".

Amendments to the Council Tax Reduction Schemes (Prescribed Requirements) (England) Regulations 2012

8.–(1) The Council Tax Reduction Schemes (Prescribed Requirements) (England) Regulations 2012 are amended as follows.
(2) In regulation 2 (interpretation), in paragraph (1) after the definition of "member of a couple" insert–

""member of the work-related activity group" means a claimant who has or is treated as having limited capability for work under either–
(a) Part 5 of the Employment and Support Allowance Regulations 2008 other than by virtue of regulation 30 of those Regulations; or
(b) Part 4 of the Employment and Support Allowance Regulations 2013 other than by virtue of regulation 26 of those Regulations;".

(3) In Schedule 1 (pensioners: matters that must be included in an authority's scheme), in paragraph 25 (treatment of child care charges), in sub-paragraph (10)(c)–
(a) omit "or the work-related activity component";
(b) after "limited capability for work" insert "or the other member of the couple would be a member of the work-related activity group".
(4) In Schedule 4 (sums disregarded from the applicant's earnings), in paragraph 5, in sub-paragraph (1)(d)(ii) omit the words "or the work-related activity component".

SCHEDULE 2

Transitional and savings provisions
PART 1
Employment and Support Allowance: transitional and savings provisions

Transitional and savings provisions: General

1.–(1) The amendments made by regulations 2 and 3, paragraphs 1 to 9 of Schedule 1 and by section 15(1) to (3) of the Welfare Reform and Work Act 2016 (which amend sections 2 and 4 of the Welfare Reform Act 2007) do not apply where any of the circumstances in paragraphs 2 to 7 apply.
(2) In this Part–
"assessment phase" has the same meaning as in the Welfare Reform Act 2007;
"a claim" means making a claim for an employment and support allowance in accordance with regulations 4ZC, 4G, 4H and 4I of the Social Security (Claims and Payments) Regulations 1987 or regulations 13 to 17 of the Universal Credit, Personal Independence Payment, Jobseeker's Allowance and Employment and Support Allowance (Claims and Payments) Regulations 2013;
"employment and support allowance" means an allowance under Part 1 of the Welfare Reform Act 2007;
"ESA Regulations 2008" means the Employment and Support Allowance Regulations 2008;
"ESA Regulations 2013" means the Employment and Support Allowance Regulations 2013.

Claimants who have made a claim for employment and support allowance before 3rd April 2017

2. The first circumstance is where the claimant has made or is treated as having made a claim for an employment and support allowance before 3rd April 2017 and that claim results in an award of employment and support allowance.

Claimants who had been found to have limited capability for work before 3rd April 2017

3. The second circumstance is where the claimant's period of limited capability for work began on or after 3rd April 2017 and is treated as a continuation of an earlier period of limited capability for work which began before 3rd April 2017 by virtue of–
(a) regulation 145 of the ESA Regulations 2008; or
(b) regulation 86 of the ESA Regulations 2013.

Claimants on Incapacity Benefits who have or will become notified persons

4. The third circumstance is where the claimant is or becomes a notified person within the meaning of regulation 4 of the Employment and Support Allowance (Transitional Provisions, Housing Benefit and Council Tax Benefit) (Existing Awards) (No. 2) Regulations 2010 and a determination is effective as to whether that person–

ESA and UC (Miscellaneous Amendments and Transitional and Savings Provisions) Regulations 2017

(a) has or is to be treated as having limited capability for work under Part 5 of the ESA Regulations 2008;
(b) has or is to be treated as having limited capability for work under Part 5 of the ESA Regulations 2013;
(c) has or is to be treated as having limited capability for work-related activity under Part 6 of the ESA Regulations 2008; or
(d) has or is to be treated as having limited capability for work-related activity under Part 6 of the ESA Regulations 2013.

Claimants where their award becomes payable before 3rd April 2017
5. The fourth circumstance is where the claimant becomes entitled to an employment and support allowance before 3rd April 2017 by virtue of–
(a) regulation 19(1) and paragraph 16 of Schedule 4 to the Social Security (Claims and Payments) Regulations 1987; or
(b) regulation 28 of the Universal Credit, Personal Independence Payment, Jobseeker's Allowance and Employment and Support Allowance (Claims and Payments) Regulations 2013.

Claimants where their assessment phase begins before 3rd April 2017
6. The fifth circumstance is where the first day of the claimant's assessment phase began before 3rd April 2017 by virtue of–
(a) regulation 5 of the ESA Regulations 2008; or
(b) regulation 6 of the ESA Regulations 2013.

Claimants where they have been entitled to maternity allowance
7. The sixth circumstance is where–
(a) a claimant was entitled to a maternity allowance under section 35 of the Social Security Contributions and Benefits Act 1992 and the end of that award is within 12 weeks beginning with the date that the claim for an employment and support allowance is made; and
(b) immediately prior to their entitlement to a maternity allowance beginning the claimant was previously entitled to an employment and support allowance before 3rd April 2017.

PART 2
Universal Credit: transitional and savings provisions

Transitional and savings provisions: General
8.–(1) The amendments made by regulations 4 and 5 and paragraphs 13, 16 and 17 of Schedule 1 do not apply–
(a) where a claimant has an award of universal credit in any of the circumstances in the following paragraphs; and
(b) for so long as the claimant continues to be entitled to universal credit and to have limited capability for work.
(2) For the purposes of sub-paragraph (1)(b), the reference to continuous entitlement to universal credit includes where an award has terminated and a further award is made and–
(a) immediately before the further award commences, the previous award has terminated because the claimant ceased to be a member of a couple or became a member of a couple; or
(b) within the six months beginning with the date that the further award commences, the previous award has terminated because the financial condition in section 5(1)(b) or, if it was a joint claim, section 5(2)(b), of the Welfare Reform Act 2012 was not met.
(3) In this Part–
"employment and support allowance" means an employment and support allowance under Part 1 of the Welfare Reform Act 2007;
"LCW element" and "LCWRA element" have the meanings in regulation 27 of the Universal Credit Regulations 2013 as it has effect apart from the amendments made by regulation 4(4) (which remove references to the LCW element);
"limited capability for work" has the meaning given in section 37(1) of the Welfare Reform Act 2012.
(4) The Universal Credit, Personal Independence Payment, Jobseeker's Allowance and Employment and Support Allowance (Claims and Payments) Regulations 2013 apply for the purpose of deciding the date on which a claim for universal credit is made or is to be treated as made.

Claimants entitled to the LCW element before 3rd April 2017
9. The first circumstance is where immediately before 3rd April 2017 the award included the LCW element, or would have but for regulation 28(1) of the Universal Credit Regulations 2013, as it has effect apart from the amendments made by regulation 4(5)(a) (which removes the reference to the LCW element).

Claimants entitled to the LCWRA element before 3rd April 2017
10. The second circumstance is where–

(a) immediately before 3rd April 2017 the award included the LCWRA element;
(b) on or after 3rd April 2017 a determination that the claimant has limited capability for work is made; and
(c) the claimant had limited capability for work and work-related activity throughout the period beginning immediately before 3rd April 2017 and ending with the date on which the determination that the claimant has limited capability for work is made.

Claimants who are providing evidence of having limited capability for work before 3rd April 2017
11. The third circumstance is where–
(a) before 3rd April 2017–
   (i) it falls to be determined whether the claimant has limited capability for work; and
   (ii) the claimant has provided evidence of having limited capability for work in accordance with the Social Security (Medical Evidence) Regulations 1976; and
(b) on or after 3rd April 2017 a determination that the claimant has limited capability for work is made on the basis of an assessment under Part 5 of the Universal Credit Regulations 2013, on revision under section 9 of the Social Security Act 1998 or on appeal.

Claimants who appeal or seek revision of a decision relating to employment and support allowance
12. The fourth circumstance is where–
(a) the claimant appeals or seeks revision under section 9 of the Social Security Act 1998 of a decision relating to the entitlement of the claimant to an employment and support allowance, where the claim for employment and support allowance was made or treated as made before 3rd April 2017; and
(b) on or after 3rd April 2017, in accordance with article 24 of the Welfare Reform Act 2012 (Commencement No 9 and Transitional and Transitory Provisions and Commencement No 8 and Savings and Transitional Provisions (Amendment)) Order 2013, the Secretary of State considers it appropriate to revise under section 9 of the Social Security Act 1998 an award of universal credit so as to include the LCW element.

Claimants entitled to employment and support allowance before 3rd April 2017
13. The fifth circumstance is where immediately before 3rd April 2017 the claimant was entitled to employment and support allowance and remains so entitled throughout the period beginning with 3rd April 2017 and ending with the date on which the claim for universal credit is made or treated as made.

Claimants entitled to be credited with earnings under the Social Security (Credits) Regulations 1975 before 3rd April 2017
14. The sixth circumstance is where–
(a) immediately before 3rd April 2017–
   (i) the claimant entitled to the award was entitled to be credited with earnings equal to the lower earnings limit then in force in respect of a week to which regulation 8B(2)(a)(iv), (iva) or (v) of the Social Security (Credits) Regulations 1975 applies; and
   (ii) paragraph 13 does not apply to that claimant; and
(b) the claimant is so entitled in respect of each week that falls in the period beginning with 3rd April 2017 and ending with the date on which the claim for universal credit is made or treated as made.

Claimants entitled to income support or other incapacity benefits before 3rd April 2017
15. The seventh circumstance is where regulation 22, 23, 24, 26 or 27 of the Universal Credit (Transitional Provisions) Regulations 2014 applies to the claimant throughout the period beginning immediately before 3rd April 2017 and ending with the date on which the claim for universal credit is made or treated as made.

The Housing Benefit and Universal Credit (Size Criteria) (Miscellaneous Amendments) Regulations 2017

(2017 No.213)

Made 27th February 2017
Laid before Parliament 2nd March 2017
Coming into force 1st April 2017

The Secretary of State for Work and Pensions makes the following Regulations in exercise of the powers conferred by sections 123(1)(d), 130A(2) to (5), 137(1) and 175(1), (3), (4) and (5) of the Social Security Contributions and Benefits Act 1992, section 122(1) and (6)(b) of the Housing Act 1996 and sections 11(4) and 42(2) and (3) of the Welfare Reform Act 2012.

In accordance with section 173(1)(b) of the Social Security Administration Act 1992, the Social Security Advisory Committee has agreed that proposals in respect of these Regulations should not be referred to it.

In respect of provisions relating to housing benefit, in accordance with section 176(1) of the Social Security Administration Act 1992 the Secretary of State has consulted with organisations appearing to him to be representative of the authorities concerned.

Citation, commencement and transitional provision

1.–(1) These Regulations may be cited as the Housing Benefit and Universal Credit (Size Criteria) (Miscellaneous Amendments) Regulations 2017 and come into force on 1st April 2017.

(2)-(3) *[Omitted]*

Amendments to the Rent Officers (Housing Benefit Functions) Order 1997

2.–(1) Schedule 2 (size criteria) to the Rent Officers (Housing Benefit Functions) Order 1997 is amended as follows.

(2) In paragraph 1–
(a) before sub-paragraph (a) insert–

"(za) a member of a couple who cannot share a bedroom;
(zb) a member of a couple who can share a bedroom;";

(b) in sub-paragraph (a) omit "(within the meaning of Part VII of the Social Security Contributions and Benefits Act 1992)";
(c) in the full-out words at the end–
  (i) after "a child who cannot share a bedroom" insert "or a member of a couple who cannot share a bedroom";
  (ii) after "the child" insert "or the member of the couple".

(3) In paragraph 1A, for sub-paragraph (a) substitute–

"(a) one or more of the following persons is stated as being a person who requires overnight care–
  (i) the tenant;
  (ii) the tenant's partner;
  (iii) a person (other than the tenant or the tenant's partner) who occupies the dwelling as their home;
  (iv) a child or young person in respect of whom the tenant or the tenant's partner is a qualifying parent or carer; or".

(4) In paragraph 3–
(a) after "child who cannot share a bedroom" insert ", "couple", "member of a couple who cannot share a bedroom";

(b) at the end insert "and reference to a member of a couple who can share a bedroom is to be construed in accordance with regulation 2(6) of those Regulations".

Amendments to the Rent Officers (Housing Benefit Functions) (Scotland) Order 1997

3.–(1) Schedule 2 (size criteria) to the Rent Officers (Housing Benefit Functions) (Scotland) Order 1997 is amended as follows.
(2) In paragraph 1–
(a) before sub-paragraph (a) insert–

"(za) a member of a couple who cannot share a bedroom;
(zb) a member of a couple who can share a bedroom;";

(b) in sub-paragraph (a) omit "(within the meaning of Part VII of the Social Security Contributions and Benefits Act 1992)";
(c) in the full-out words at the end–
  (i) after "a child who cannot share a bedroom" insert "or a member of a couple who cannot share a bedroom";
  (ii) after "the child" insert "or the member of the couple".
(3) In paragraph 1A, for sub-paragraph (a) substitute–

"(a) one or more of the following persons is stated as being a person who requires overnight care–
  (i) the tenant;
  (ii) the tenant's partner;
  (iii) a person (other than the tenant or the tenant's partner) who occupies the dwelling as their home;
  (iv) a child or young person in respect of whom the tenant or the tenant's partner is a qualifying parent or carer; or".

(4) In paragraph 3–
(a) after "child who cannot share a bedroom" insert ", "couple", "member of a couple who cannot share a bedroom";
(b) at the end insert "and reference to a member of a couple who can share a bedroom is to be construed in accordance with regulation 2(6) of those Regulations".

Amendments to the Housing Benefit Regulations 2006

4.–(1) The Housing Benefit Regulations 2006 are amended as follows.
(2) In regulation 2 (interpretation)–
(a) after the definition of "maximum rent (LHA)" insert–

""member of a couple who cannot share a bedroom" means a member of a couple–
(a) who is in receipt of–
  (i) attendance allowance at the higher rate in accordance with section 65(3) of the Act;
  (ii) the care component of disability living allowance at the highest or middle rate prescribed in accordance with section 72(3) of the Act;
  (iii) the daily living component of personal independence payment in accordance with section 78 of the 2012 Act; or
  (iv) armed forces independence payment; and
(b) whom the relevant authority is satisfied is, by virtue of his or her disability, not reasonably able to share a bedroom with the other member of the couple;";

(b) in the definition of "person who requires overnight care" in paragraph (a)(iii) after "provided" insert "or, where P is a child, the claimant has provided";

(c) after paragraph (5) insert–

"(6) For the purpose of these Regulations, reference to a member of a couple who can share a bedroom is to a member of a couple where the other member of the couple is a member of a couple who cannot share a bedroom.".

(3) In regulation B13 (determination of a maximum rent (social sector))–
(a) in paragraph (5)–
  (i) before sub-paragraph (a) insert–

"(za) a member of a couple who cannot share a bedroom;
(zb) a member of a couple who can share a bedroom;";

  (ii) in sub-paragraph (a) omit "(within the meaning of Part 7 of the Act)";
(b) in paragraph (6), for sub-paragraph (a) substitute–

"(a) one or more relevant persons in paragraph (9)(a), (b) or (e) is a person who requires overnight care;
(ab) one or more relevant persons in paragraph (9)(c) or (d) is a person who requires overnight care; or";

(c) in paragraph (7), in sub-paragraph (b), for "a sub-paragraph of paragraph (6)" substitute "paragraph (6)(b)";
(d) in paragraph (9), after sub-paragraph (d) insert–

"(e) for the purposes of paragraph (6)(a)–
  (i) a person (other than the claimant, the claimant's partner, P or P's partner) who occupies the claimant's dwelling as their home;
  (ii) a child or young person in respect of whom a relevant person under sub-paragraphs (a) to (e)(i) is a qualifying parent or carer.".

(4) In regulation 13D (determination of a maximum rent (LHA))–
(a) in paragraph (3)–
  (i) before sub-paragraph (a) insert–

"(za) a member of a couple who cannot share a bedroom;
(zb) a member of a couple who can share a bedroom;";

  (ii) in sub-paragraph (a) omit "(within the meaning of Part 7 of the Act)";
  (iii) in the full-out words at the end–
    (aa) after "a child who cannot share a bedroom" insert "or a member of a couple who cannot share a bedroom";
    (bb) after "the child" insert "or the member of the couple".
(b) in paragraph (3A), for sub-paragraph (a) substitute–

"(a) one or more of the following persons is a person who requires overnight care–
  (i) the claimant;
  (ii) the claimant's partner;
  (iii) a person (other than the claimant or the claimant's partner) who occupies the claimant's dwelling as their home;
  (iv) a child or young person in respect of whom the claimant or the claimant's partner is a qualifying parent or carer; or".

(5) In regulation 114A (information to be provided to rent officers), in paragraph (9)(ca), for "the claimant or the claimant's partner" substitute "any person mentioned in regulation 13D(3A)(a)".

(6) In Schedule 2 (excluded tenancies), in paragraph 2(3)–

(a) for paragraph (f) substitute–

"(f) any person mentioned in paragraph 1A(a) of Schedule 2 to the Rent Officers Order becomes or ceases to be a person who requires overnight care where that affects the size criteria, as set out in that Schedule to that Order, applicable in the claimant's case;";

(b) in paragraph (h) after "child who cannot share a bedroom" insert "or a member of a couple who cannot share a bedroom".

Amendments to the Housing Benefit (Persons who have attained the qualifying age for state pension credit) Regulations 2006

5.–(1) The Housing Benefit (Persons who have attained the qualifying age for state pension credit) Regulations 2006 are amended as follows.

(2) In regulation 2 (interpretation)–
(a) after the definition of "maximum rent (LHA)" insert–

""member of a couple who cannot share a bedroom" means a member of a couple–
(a) who is in receipt of–
    (i) attendance allowance at the higher rate in accordance with section 65(3) of the Act;
    (ii) the care component of disability living allowance at the highest or middle rate prescribed in accordance with section 72(3) of the Act;
    (iii) the daily living component of personal independence payment in accordance with section 78 of the 2012 Act; or
    (iv) armed forces independence payment; and
(b) whom the relevant authority is satisfied is, by virtue of his or her disability, not reasonably able to share a bedroom with the other member of the couple;";

(b) in the definition of "person who requires overnight care" in paragraph (a)(iii) after "provided" insert "or, where P is a child, the claimant has provided";
(c) after paragraph (6) insert–

"(7) For the purpose of these Regulations, reference to a member of a couple who can share a bedroom is to a member of a couple where the other member of the couple is a member of a couple who cannot share a bedroom.".

(3) In regulation 13D (determination of a maximum rent (LHA))–
(a) in paragraph (3)–
    (i) before sub-paragraph (a) insert–

"(za) a member of a couple who cannot share a bedroom;
(zb) a member of a couple who can share a bedroom;";

   (ii) in sub-paragraph (a) omit "(within the meaning of Part 7 of the Act)";
   (iii) in the full-out words at the end–
        (aa) after "a child who cannot share a bedroom" insert "or a member of a couple who cannot share a bedroom";
        (bb) after "the child" insert "or the member of the couple".
(b) in paragraph (3A), for sub-paragraph (a) substitute–

"(a) one or more of the following persons is a person who requires overnight care–
    (i) the claimant;
    (ii) the claimant's partner;
    (iii) a person (other than the claimant or the claimant's partner) who occupies the claimant's dwelling as their home;

(iv) a child or young person in respect of whom the claimant or the claimant's partner is a qualifying parent or carer; or".

(4) In regulation 95A (information to be provided to rent officers), in paragraph (9)(ba), for "the claimant or the claimant's partner" substitute "any person mentioned in regulation 13D(3A)(a)".

(5) In Schedule 2 (excluded tenancies), in paragraph 2(3)–

(a) for paragraph (e) substitute–

"(e) any person mentioned in paragraph 1A(a) of Schedule 2 to the Rent Officers Order becomes or ceases to be a person who requires overnight care where that affects the size criteria, as set out in that Schedule to that Order, applicable in the claimant's case;";

(b) in paragraph (g) after "child who cannot share a bedroom" insert "or a member of a couple who cannot share a bedroom".

The Social Security (Scottish Infected Blood Support Scheme) Regulations 2017

(2017 No.329)

Made	8th March 2017
Laid before Parliament	13th March 2017
Coming into force	3rd April 2017

The Secretary of State for Work and Pensions, in exercise of the powers conferred by sections 123(1)(a) and (d), 136(3) and (5), 136A(3), 137(1) and 175(1) and (3) of the Social Security Contributions and Benefits Act 1992, section 189(4) of the Social Security Administration Act 1992, sections 12(1) and (4), 35(1) and 36(2) of the Jobseekers Act 1995, sections 29 and 30(4) and paragraph 8 of Schedule 1 to the Social Security (Recovery of Benefits) Act 1997, sections 15(3) and (6)(b) and 17(1) of the State Pension Credit Act 2002 and sections 17(1) and (3), 24(1) and 25(3) of the Welfare Reform Act 2007, makes the following Regulations.

In accordance with section 173(1)(b) of the Social Security Administration Act 1992, the Social Security Advisory Committee agreed that the proposals in respect of these Regulations should not be referred to it.

In respect of the provisions in these Regulations relating to housing benefit, in accordance with section 176(1) of the Social Security Administration Act 1992, the Secretary of State has consulted with organisations appearing to him to be representative of the authorities concerned.

Citation and commencement

1. These Regulations may be cited as the Social Security (Scottish Infected Blood Support Scheme) Regulations 2017 and come into force on 3rd April 2017.

Amendments to the Housing Benefit Regulations 2006

6.–(1) The Housing Benefit Regulations 2006 are amended as follows.
(2) In regulation 2(1) (interpretation)–
(a) in the definition of "qualifying person", after "the Caxton Foundation" insert ", the Scottish Infected Blood Support Scheme";
(b) after the definition of "Scottish basic rate" insert–

""Scottish Infected Blood Support Scheme" means the scheme of that name administered by the Common Services Agency (constituted by section 10 of the National Health Service (Scotland) Act 1978);".

(3) In each of the following provisions, after "the Caxton Foundation" insert ", the Scottish Infected Blood Support Scheme"–
(a) regulation 42(7)(a) (notional income);
(b) regulation 46(6) (income treated as capital);
(c) regulation 49(4)(a) (notional capital);
(d) regulation 74(9)(b) (non-dependant deductions);
(e) regulation 86(4)(a)(ii) (evidence and information);
(f) paragraphs 35(1) and (7) of Schedule 5 (sums to be disregarded in the calculation of income);
(g) paragraphs 24(1) and (7) and 34 of Schedule 6 (capital to be disregarded).

Amendments to the Housing Benefit (Persons who have attained the qualifying age for state pension credit) Regulations 2006

7.–(1) The Housing Benefit (Persons who have attained the qualifying age for state pension credit) Regulations 2006 are amended as follows.
(2) In regulation 2(1) (interpretation)–

The Social Security (Scottish Infected Blood Support Scheme) Regulations 2017

(a) in the definition of "qualifying person", after "the Caxton Foundation" insert ", the Scottish Infected Blood Support Scheme";
(b) after the definition of "Scottish basic rate" insert–

""Scottish Infected Blood Support Scheme" means the scheme of that name administered by the Common Services Agency (constituted by section 10 of the National Health Service (Scotland) Act 1978);".

(3) In each of the following provisions, after "the Caxton Foundation" insert ", the Scottish Infected Blood Support Scheme"–
(a) regulation 55(10)(b) (non-dependant deductions);
(b) regulation 67(4)(a)(ii) (evidence and information);
(c) paragraph 16(1)(a) of Schedule 6 (capital to be disregarded).

The Social Security (Restrictions on Amounts for Children and Qualifying Young Persons) Amendment Regulations 2017

(2017 No.376)

Made	13th March 2017
Laid before Parliament	15th March 2017
Coming into force	6th April 2017

The Secretary of State, in exercise of the powers conferred by sections 123(1)(a) and (d), 135(1), 136(3) and (5)(b), 137 and 175(1), (3) and (4) of the Social Security Contributions and Benefits Act 1992, sections 4(5), 12(1) and (4)(b), 35 and 36(2) of the Jobseekers Act 1995, sections 4(5)(b), 10(4), 11(3)(b) and (c), 12(1) and (4)(b), 19(2)(d), 20(1)(b), 24(5), 40 and 42(1), (2) and (3) of, and paragraphs 4(1)(a) and (3)(a) and 5(1) of Schedule 1 and paragraphs 1(1) and 3(1)(b) of Schedule 6 to, the Welfare Reform Act 2012 and sections 14(6) and 34 of the Welfare Reform and Work Act 2016, makes the following Regulations.

This instrument contains only regulations made under, by virtue of, or consequential upon, sections 13 and 14 of the Welfare Reform and Work Act 2016 and is made before the end of the period of 6 months beginning with the coming into force of those sections. Therefore, in accordance with section 173(5) of the Social Security Administration Act 1992, these Regulations are not required to be referred to the Social Security Advisory Committee.

In respect of the provisions in these Regulations relating to housing benefit, in accordance with section 176(1) of the Social Security Administration Act 1992, the Secretary of State has consulted with organisations appearing to him to be representative of the authorities concerned.

Citation and commencement

1. These Regulations may be cited as the Social Security (Restrictions on Amounts for Children and Qualifying Young Persons) Amendment Regulations 2017 and come into force on 6th April 2017.

Minor amendment consequential on restriction on claims for universal credit by persons with more than two children

4. In paragraph (2) of article 7 (transitional provision: claims for housing benefit, income support or a tax credit) of the Welfare Reform Act 2012 (Commencement No. 23 and Transitional and Transitory Provisions) Order 2015, after "regulation 4" insert ", or by virtue of regulation 39,".

Restrictions on amounts for children and young persons – consequential changes to housing benefit

7.–(1) The Housing Benefit Regulations 2006 are amended as follows.
(2) In regulation 22 (applicable amounts)–
(a) the existing text becomes paragraph (1) and for sub-paragraph (b) (of that paragraph (1)) substitute–

"(b) an amount determined in accordance with paragraph 2 of Schedule 3 in respect of up to two individuals who are either children or young persons and who are members of his family;"; and

(b) at the end insert–

"(2) For the purposes of paragraph (1)(b), as it applies apart from paragraph (4), where the family includes more than two individuals who are either children or young persons, and, under paragraph 2 of Schedule 3, a different amount applies to different individuals, the two amounts to be included in the applicable amount shall be those that result in the greatest possible total amount.

(3) Paragraph (4) applies where–
(a) (whether or not as part of a tax credit couple) the claimant has an award of child tax credit in respect of a child or young person who is a member of his family, and whether or not any amount is payable by way of such credit; and
(b) the total amount to be included in the applicable amount under paragraph (1)(b) as substituted by paragraph (4) would be higher than the total amount that would be included under paragraph (1)(b) apart from paragraph (4).
(4) Where this paragraph applies, for paragraph (1)(b) substitute–
"(b) an amount determined in accordance with paragraph 2 of Schedule 3 in respect of any child or young person who is a member of his family and in respect of whom the individual element of child tax credit has been included in the determination of the maximum rate of that credit;".
(5) In this regulation, "tax credit couple" means a couple as defined in section 3(5A) of the Tax Credits Act 2002.".

(3) In regulation 23 (polygamous marriages)–
(a) the existing text becomes paragraph (1) and for sub-paragraph (c) (of that paragraph (1)) substitute–

"(c) an amount determined in accordance with paragraph 2 of Schedule 3 in respect of up to two individuals who are either children or young persons and for whom he or a partner of his is responsible and who are members of the same household;"; and

(b) at the end insert–

"(2) For the purposes of paragraph (1)(c), as it applies apart from paragraph (4), where the claimant and his partners are between them responsible for more than two individuals who are either children or young persons and who are members of the same household, and, under paragraph 2 of Schedule 3, a different amount applies to different individuals, the two amounts to be included in the applicable amount shall be those that result in the greatest possible total amount.
(3) Paragraph (4) applies where–
(a) (as part of a polygamous unit) the claimant has an award of child tax credit in respect of any child or young person for whom he or a partner of his is responsible and who is a member of the same household, and whether or not any amount is payable by way of such credit; and
(b) the total amount to be included in the applicable amount under paragraph (1)(c) as substituted by paragraph (4) would be higher than the total amount that would be included under paragraph (1)(c) apart from paragraph (4).
(4) Where this paragraph applies, for paragraph (1)(c) substitute–
"(c) an amount determined in accordance with paragraph 2 of Schedule 3 in respect of any child or young person for whom he or a partner of his is responsible and who is a member of the same household and in respect of whom the individual element of child tax credit has been included in the determination of the maximum rate of that credit;".
(5) In this regulation, "polygamous unit" has the same meaning as in regulation 2 of the Tax Credits (Polygamous Marriages) Regulations 2003.".

(4) In paragraphs 1, 2(1), 4 and 30(4) of Schedule 3 (applicable amounts), after "22" and "23", in each place where they occur, insert "(1)".

Restrictions on amounts for children and young persons – consequential changes to housing benefit for persons over state pension credit age
8.–(1) The Housing Benefit (Persons who have attained the qualifying age for state pension credit) Regulations 2006 are amended as follows.
(2) In regulation 22 (applicable amounts)–

(a) for sub-paragraph (b) of paragraph (1) substitute–

"(b) an amount determined in accordance with paragraph 2 of that Schedule in respect of up to two individuals who are either children or young persons and who are members of his family;"; and

(b) at the end insert–

"(5A) For the purposes of paragraph (1)(b), as it applies apart from paragraph (5C), where the family includes more than two individuals who are either children or young persons, and, under paragraph 2 of that Schedule, a different amount applies to different individuals, the two amounts to be included in the applicable amount shall be those that result in the greatest possible total amount.
(5B) Paragraph (5C) applies where–
(a) (whether or not as part of a tax credit couple) the claimant has an award of child tax credit in respect of a child or young person who is a member of his family, whether or not any amount is payable by way of such credit; and
(b) the total amount to be included in the applicable amount under paragraph (1)(b) as substituted by paragraph (5C) would be higher than the total amount that would be included under paragraph (1)(b) apart from paragraph (5C).
(5C) Where this paragraph applies, for paragraph (1)(b) substitute–
"(b) an amount determined in accordance with paragraph 2 of that Schedule in respect of any child or young person who is a member of his family and in respect of whom the individual element of child tax credit has been included in the determination of the maximum rate of that credit;".
(5D) In this regulation, "tax credit couple" means a couple as defined in section 3(5A) of the Tax Credits Act 2002.".

Housing Benefit – transitional provisions for restrictions on amounts for children and young persons

9.–(1) This regulation applies where, on 5th April 2017, a person is entitled to housing benefit and the person is, or the person and the person's partner are between them, responsible for more than two individuals who are either children or young persons and who are members of the same household (each such individual is referred to as a "protected individual").
(2) Where this regulation applies, the amendments made by regulations 7 and 8 do not apply to the person entitled to housing benefit referred to in paragraph (1) until–
(a) the person makes a new claim for housing benefit; or
(b) the person or the person's partner (if any) becomes responsible for a new individual,
whichever is the first to occur.
(3) Paragraphs (4) to (8) apply where–
(a) the amendments made by regulations 7 and 8 apply by virtue of paragraph (2)(b);
(b) the child tax credit provisions do not apply; and
(c) the person has not made a new claim for housing benefit.
(4) Notwithstanding the default provisions, a child amount shall be included in the applicable amount in relation to any protected individual, in relation to any time when the person or the person's partner (if any) is responsible for the individual and the individual is a member of the same household.
(5) Paragraph (6) applies where–
(a) the person or the person's partner (if any) is responsible for one or more protected individuals who are members of the same household; and
(b) either of them is responsible for one or more new individuals who are members of the same household.
(6) Where this paragraph applies, any protected individual for whom the person or the person's partner is responsible is to be counted for the purpose of deciding whether,

under the default provisions, an additional child amount is to be included in the applicable amount with respect to the new individual or individuals referred to in paragraph (5)(b).

(7) Paragraph (8) applies where–
(a) the number of protected individuals for whom either the person or the person's partner (if any) is responsible, and who are members of the same household, is one;
(b) the number of new individuals for whom either the person or the person's partner is responsible, and who are members of the same household, is two or more; and
(c) a different child amount would apply to different individuals.

(8) Where this paragraph applies, the child amounts to be included in the applicable amount shall be–
(a) the child amount in relation to the protected individual; and
(b) a child amount in relation to such one of the new individuals as will result in the greatest possible total amount.

(9) Under paragraph (3), for the purposes of determining whether the child tax credit provisions apply, by virtue of regulation 22(3) or 23(3) of the 2006 Regulations or regulation 22(5B) of the 2006 (SPC) Regulations, where the person or the person's partner is responsible for one or more protected individuals, the total amount that would be included in the applicable amount under the default provisions shall be taken to be the total that would be included under paragraphs (4), (6) and (8).

(10) For the purposes of this regulation–
(a) "the 2006 Regulations" means the Housing Benefit Regulations 2006 and "the 2006 (SPC) Regulations" means the Housing Benefit (Persons who have attained the qualifying age for state pension credit) Regulations 2006;
(b) "applicable amount" has the same meaning as in section 135 of the Social Security Contributions and Benefits Act 1992;
(c) "child", "partner" and "young person" have the same meanings as in the 2006 Regulations;
(d) "child amount" means the amount determined under whichever is relevant of paragraph 2 of Schedule 3 to the 2006 Regulations or paragraph 2 of Schedule 3 to the 2006 (SPC) Regulations;
(e) "child tax credit provisions" means whichever is relevant of regulation 22(1)(b) or 23(1)(c) of the 2006 Regulations or regulation 22(1)(b) of the 2006 (SPC) Regulations, as substituted by regulation 22(4) or 23(4) of the 2006 Regulations or regulation 22(5C) of the 2006 (SPC) Regulations respectively;
(f) "default provisions" means whichever is relevant of regulation 22(1)(b) or 23(1)(c) of the 2006 Regulations or regulation 22(1)(b) of the 2006 (SPC) Regulations, as they apply apart from regulation 22(4) or 23(4) of the 2006 Regulations or regulation 22(5C) of the 2006 (SPC) Regulations respectively;
(g) "new individual" means a child or young person who is not a protected individual;
(h) any reference to an individual being part of the same household means being part of the same household with the person who is entitled to housing benefit and the person's partner (if any);
(i) a person is to be treated as responsible for a child or young person in the circumstances set out in regulation 20 of the 2006 Regulations.

The Pensions Act 2014 (Consequential, Supplementary and Incidental Amendments) Order 2017
(2017 No.422)

Made at 9.00 a.m. on 16th March 2017
Laid before Parliament at 2.00 p.m. on 16th March 2017
Coming into force in accordance with articles 1(2), 2 and 3

The Secretary of State for Work and Pensions makes the following Order in exercise of the powers conferred by sections 53 and 54(5) of the Pensions Act 2014.

Citation and commencement
1.–(1) This Order may be cited as the Pensions Act 2014 (Consequential, Supplementary and Incidental Amendments) Order 2017.
(2) This Order comes into force on the day on which section 30 of the Pensions Act 2014 (bereavement support payment) comes into force for all purposes (this is subject to articles 2 and 3).

Later commencement for abolition of bereavement payment and bereavement allowance
2.–(1) This Order does not come into force in accordance with article 1(2) for a person to whom this article applies (this is subject to article 3).
(2) This article applies to a person who, on the day before the day on which section 30 of the Pensions Act 2014 comes into force for all purposes–
(a) was entitled to–
  (i) a bereavement payment under section 36 of the Social Security Contributions and Benefits Act 1992 (bereavement payment); or
  (ii) a bereavement allowance under section 39B of that Act (bereavement allowance where no dependent children); or
(b) would have been entitled to such a benefit if they made a claim for it.
(3) But this article ceases to apply to a person if–
(a) they were entitled to a benefit in accordance with paragraph (2)(a) and they are no longer entitled to that benefit; or
(b) they would have been entitled to a benefit in accordance with paragraph (2)(b) and they would no longer be entitled to that benefit if they made a claim for it.
(4) On the date this article ceases to apply to a person, this Order comes into force for that person.

Commencement for entitlement to bereavement payment and bereavement support payment
3.–(1) This Order does not come into force in accordance with article 1(2) for a person to whom this article applies.
(2) This article applies to a person–
(a) whose spouse or civil partner died in the 12 months before the day on which section 30 of the Pensions Act 2014 came into force for all purposes;
(b) who would have been entitled to a bereavement payment under section 36 of the Social Security Contributions and Benefits Act 1992 if they had made a claim for it;
(c) who formed a new marriage or civil partnership; and
(d) whose new spouse or civil partner died–
  (i) on or after the day on which section 30 of the Pensions Act 2014 came into force for all purposes; and
  (ii) within 12 months of the death referred to in sub-paragraph (a).
(3) This Order comes into force for a person to whom this article applies–

(a) at the end of the period of 12 months starting on the day on which the death referred to in paragraph (2)(a) occurred, for the purposes of entitlement to bereavement payment for the death referred to in paragraph (2)(a); and

(b) on the day on which section 30 of the Pensions Act 2014 comes into force for all purposes, for the purposes of entitlement to bereavement support payment for the death referred to in paragraph (2)(d).

Amendment of the Housing Benefit Regulations 2006

25.–(1) The Housing Benefit Regulations 2006 are amended as follows.

(2) In Schedule 5 (sums to be disregarded in the calculation of income other than earnings), after paragraph 66 insert–

"67. Any bereavement support payment under section 30 of the Pensions Act 2014 (bereavement support payment) except any such payment which is disregarded as capital under paragraph 9(1)(h) or 62 of Schedule 6.".

(3) In Schedule 6 (capital to be disregarded)–
(a) in paragraph 9(1), after paragraph (g) insert–

"(h) bereavement support payment under section 30 of the Pensions Act 2014,"; and

(b) after paragraph 61, insert–

"62. Any bereavement support payment in respect of the rate set out in regulation 3(2) or (5) of the Bereavement Support Payment Regulations 2017 (rate of bereavement support payment), but only for a period of 52 weeks from the date of receipt of the payment.".

Amendment of the Housing Benefit (Persons who have attained the qualifying age for State Pension Credit) Regulations 2006

26.–(1) The Housing Benefit (Persons who have attained the qualifying age for State Pension Credit) Regulations 2006 are amended as follows.

(2) In regulation 29(1)(j) (meaning of income), for paragraph (xiii) substitute–

"(xiii) bereavement support payment under section 30 of the Pensions Act 2014;".

(3) In Part 1 of Schedule 6 (capital to be disregarded generally)–
(a) in paragraph 21(2), after paragraph (o) insert–

"(p) bereavement support payment under section 30 of the Pensions Act 2014."; and

(b) after paragraph 26G, insert–

"26H. A payment of bereavement support payment in respect of the rate set out in regulation 3(2) or (5) of the Bereavement Support Payment Regulations 2017 (rate of bereavement support payment), but only for a period of 52 weeks from the date of receipt of the payment.".

Amendment of the Council Tax Reduction Schemes (Prescribed Requirements) (England) Regulations 2012

41. In paragraph 16(1)(j) of Schedule 1 to the Council Tax Reduction Schemes (Prescribed Requirements) (England) Regulations 2012 (meaning of 'income': pensioners), for sub-paragraph (xiii) substitute–

"(xiii) bereavement support payment under section 30 of the Pensions Act 2014;".

The Crown Estate Transfer Scheme 2017
(2017 No.524)

Made 31st March 2017
Coming into force in accordance with paragraph 1(2)

The Treasury, with the agreement of the Scottish Ministers, make the following Scheme in exercise of the powers conferred by section 90B of the Scotland Act 1998.

A draft of this Scheme was laid before Parliament in accordance with paragraphs 1 and 2 of Schedule 7 to the Scotland Act 1998 and approved by resolution of each House of Parliament.

Citation, commencement and extent

1.–(1) This Scheme may be cited as the Crown Estate Transfer Scheme 2017.

(2) This Scheme comes into force on the day after the day on which it is made.

(3) Subject to sub-paragraph (4), this Scheme extends to England and Wales, Scotland and Northern Ireland.

(4) An amendment made by Schedule 5 has the same extent as the enactment to which it relates.

SCHEDULE 5

CONSEQUENTIAL AMENDMENTS
PART 3
Secondary legislation

Housing Benefit Regulations 2006

102. In regulation 2(1) of the Housing Benefit Regulations 2006 (interpretation)–
 (a) in the definition of "Crown tenant", at the end insert "or a relevant person", and
 (b) insert in the appropriate place–

""relevant person", in relation to any property, rights or interests to which section 90B(5) of the Scotland Act 1998 applies, means the person who manages that property or those rights or interests;".

Housing Benefit (Persons who have attained the qualifying age for state pension credit) Regulations 2006

103. In regulation 2(1) of the Housing Benefit (Persons who have attained the qualifying age for state pension credit) Regulations 2006 (interpretation), as that regulation applies in relation to Scotland–
 (a) in the definition of "Crown tenant", at the end insert "or a relevant person", and
 (b) insert in the appropriate place–

""relevant person", in relation to any property, rights or interests to which section 90B(5) of the Scotland Act 1998 applies, means the person who manages that property or those rights or interests;".

The Employment and Support Allowance (Miscellaneous Amendments and Transitional and Savings Provision) Regulations 2017

(2017 No.581)

Made	23rd April 2017
Laid before Parliament	24th April 2017
Coming into force	23rd June 2017

The Secretary of State for Work and Pensions makes the following Regulations in exercise of the powers conferred by sections 15(4) and (5) and 34(1) of the Welfare Reform and Work Act 2016.

In accordance with section 173(5)(b) of the Social Security Administration Act 1992, this instrument contains only regulations made by virtue of, or consequential upon section 15 of the Welfare Reform and Work Act 2016 and is made before the end of the period of 6 months beginning with the coming into force of this section.

In accordance with section 176(1) of the Social Security Administration Act 1992 the Secretary of State has consulted with organisations appearing to him to be representative of the authorities concerned.

Citation and commencement
1. These Regulations may be cited as the Employment and Support Allowance (Miscellaneous Amendments and Transitional and Savings Provision) Regulations 2017 and come into force on 23rd June 2017.

Amendments to the Housing Benefit Regulations 2006
5.–(1) The Housing Benefit Regulations 2006 are amended as follows.
(2) In paragraph (1) of regulation 2 (interpretation)–
(a) in the definition for "main phase employment and support allowance" after "Welfare Reform Act" insert "or the claimant is a member of the work-related activity group, ";
(b) in the definition for "member of the work-related activity group" for "claimant" substitute "person".
(3) In paragraph (8)(c)(ii) of regulation 7 (circumstances in which a person is or is not to be treated as occupying a dwelling as his home)–
(a) omit "23 or";
(b) after "of that Schedule" insert "or the claimant or the claimant's partner is a member of the work-related activity group".
(4) In paragraph (8)(a) of regulation 74 (non-dependant deductions) for "or where the non-dependant is not a member of the work-related activity group" substitute "and where the non-dependant is not a member of the work-related activity group".
(5) In paragraph 1A(a) of Schedule 3 (applicable amounts) after "personally" insert "or the claimant is personally a member of the work-related activity group".
(6) In paragraph 17(2)(b)(iv)(bb) of Schedule 4 (sums to be disregarded in the calculation of earnings) omit "and is engaged in remunerative work for on average not less than 16 hours per week".

Amendments to the Housing Benefit (Persons who have attained the qualifying age for state pension credit) Regulations 2006
6.–(1) The Housing Benefit (Persons who have attained the qualifying age for state pension credit) Regulations 2006 are amended as follows.
(2) In paragraph (1) of regulation 2 (interpretation)–
(a) in the definition for "main phase employment and support allowance" after "Welfare Reform Act" insert "or the claimant is a member of the work-related activity group";

(b) in the definition for "member of the work-related activity group" for "claimant" substitute "person".

(3) In paragraph (8) of regulation 55 (non-dependant deductions) for "or where the non-dependant is not a member of the work-related activity group" substitute "and where the non-dependant is not a member of the work-related activity group".

Amendments to the Employment and Support Allowance and Universal Credit (Miscellaneous Amendments and Transitional and Savings Provisions) Regulations 2017

9. In Schedule 2 (transitional and savings provisions) to the Employment and Support Allowance and Universal Credit (Miscellaneous Amendments and Transitional and Savings Provisions) Regulations 2017–
- (a) in paragraph 1(2) in the definition for "a claim"–
  - (i) for ""a claim"" substitute ""claim"";
  - (ii) omit "making";
  - (iii) before "in accordance" insert "made";
- (b) in paragraph 4 (claimants on incapacity benefits who have or will become notified persons) after "where the claimant" insert "has been, ".

Transitional and savings provision

10. The amendments made by regulations 2 to 8 of these Regulations do not apply where any of the circumstances in paragraph 2 to 7 of Schedule 2 (transitional and savings provisions) to the Employment and Support Allowance and Universal Credit (Miscellaneous Amendments and Transitional and Savings Provisions) Regulations 2017, as amended by regulation 9 of these Regulations apply.

The Social Security (Emergency Funds) (Amendment) Regulations 2017

(2017 No.689)

Made	15th June 2017
Laid before Parliament	16th June 2017
Coming into force	19th June 2017

The Secretary of State for Work and Pensions makes the following Regulations in exercise of the powers conferred by sections 123(1)(a) and (d), 130A(2), 136(3) and (5), 136A(3), 137(1), 138(1)(a) and (4) and 175(1), (3) and (4) of the Social Security Contributions and Benefits Act 1992, sections 12(1) and (4), 35(1) and 36(2) and (4) of the Jobseekers Act 1995, sections 2(3)(b), 15(6)(b) and 17(1) of the State Pension Credit Act 2002, sections 17(1) and (3), 24(1) and 25(3) and (5) of the Welfare Reform Act 2007 and section 42(1) to (3) of, and paragraph 4(1) and (3) of Schedule 1 to, the Welfare Reform Act 2012.

In accordance with section 173(1)(b) of the Social Security Administration Act 1992, the Social Security Advisory Committee has agreed that the proposals in respect of these Regulations should not be referred to it.

In respect of provisions in these Regulations that relate to housing benefit, in accordance with section 176(2)(b) of the Social Security Administration Act 1992, organisations appearing to the Secretary of State to be representative of the authorities concerned have agreed that consultations should not be undertaken.

Citation and commencement

1. These Regulations may be cited as the Social Security (Emergency Funds) (Amendment) Regulations 2017 and come into force on 19th June 2017.

Amendment of the Housing Benefit Regulations 2006

6.—(1) The Housing Benefit Regulations 2006(1) are amended as follows.
(2) In regulation 2(1) (interpretation)–
(a) after the definition of "the London Bombings Relief Charitable Fund" insert–

""the London Emergencies Trust" means the company of that name (number 09928465) incorporated on 23rd December 2015 and the registered charity of that name (number 1172307) established on 28th March 2017;";

(b) in the definition of "qualifying person", after "the Scottish Infected Blood Support Scheme" insert ", the London Emergencies Trust, the We Love Manchester Emergency Fund";
(c) after the definition of "water charges" insert–

""the We Love Manchester Emergency Fund" means the registered charity of that name (number 1173260) established on 30th May 2017;".

(3) In each of the following provisions, after "the Scottish Infected Blood Support Scheme" insert ", the London Emergencies Trust, the We Love Manchester Emergency Fund"–
(a) regulation 42(7)(a) (notional income);
(b) regulation 46(6) (income treated as capital);
(c) regulation 49(4)(a) (notional capital);
(d) regulation 74(9)(b) (non-dependant deductions);
(e) regulation 86(4)(a)(ii) (evidence and information);
(f) paragraph 35(1) and (7) of Schedule 5 (sums to be disregarded in the calculation of income);
(g) paragraph 24(1) and (7) of Schedule 6 (capital to be disregarded).

(SI 2017 No.689, reg 7)

Amendment of the Housing Benefit (Persons who have attained the qualifying age for state pension credit) Regulations 2006

7.—(1) The Housing Benefit (Persons who have attained the qualifying age for state pension credit) Regulations 2006(1) are amended as follows.

(2) In regulation 2(1) (interpretation)–

(a) after the definition of "the London Bombings Relief Charitable fund" insert–

""the London Emergencies Trust" means the company of that name (number 09928465) incorporated on 23rd December 2015 and the registered charity of that name (number 1172307) established on 28th March 2017;";

(b) in the definition of "qualifying person", after "the Scottish Infected Blood Support Scheme" insert ", the London Emergencies Trust, the We Love Manchester Emergency Fund";

(c) after the definition of "water charges" insert–

""the We Love Manchester Emergency Fund" means the registered charity of that name (number 1173260) established on 30th May 2017;".

(3) In each of the following provisions, after "the Scottish Infected Blood Support Scheme" insert ", the London Emergencies Trust, the We Love Manchester Emergency Fund"–

(a) regulation 55(10)(b) (non-dependant deductions);
(b) regulation 67(4)(a)(ii) (evidence and information);
(c) paragraph 16(1)(a) of Schedule 6 (capital to be disregarded generally).